The

*F*AITHFUL

BAPTIST

*W*ITNESS

By

Dr. Phil Stringer

ISBN 978-0-9822230-6-2

Phil Stringer
5846 N. Kimball
Chicago, IL 60659
Phone: (773) 478-6083
Email: philstringer@att.net

All Scripture Quotations are from the
Authorized Version of the Bible.

Cover Design and Format by:
The Old Paths Publications, Inc.
Cleveland, Georgia, 30528
Phone: (706) 865-0153
Email: TOP@theoldpathspublications.com

Printed in the USA by Lightning Source, Inc.
http://www.lightningsource.com/

1.0

Table of Contents

FOREWORD

The Lord allowed my path to cross with Dr. Phil Stringer through his Baptist History lectures. I was encouraged by his well-researched presentation of our Baptist History and the New Testament Baptist Distinctives. We have used his material to help disciple young believers and strengthen older believers as to why we are Baptists. It is absolutely essential to understand why we hold to these truths.

In my experience as a Baptist preacher, I am greatly concerned by the ignorance of Baptist Church members who have little or no foundation as to why they are Baptist. The comment is often made that "I have just always been a Baptist." Weak church members become easy prey for cults and false religions in a time of trial. My father, a strong local church Baptist pastor, used to say, "I am Baptist by conviction; I was not raised this way!"

In this day, when pastors are struggling with their own churches and being bombarded by the so-called success of non-Baptist church growth, I strongly recommend *The Faithful Baptist Witness* by Dr. Phil Stringer.

May our children and our converts learn our rich history and the foundation of the New Testament Baptist Distinctives. My prayer is that they will embrace them and continue with grace and conviction.

Pastor Chris Staub
Silvery Lane Baptist Church

Dedication

This book is dedicated to my loving wife,
Cindy.

Thanks for being so understanding while I was browsing through used bookstores; for being so gracious while I was spending our money on books that I deemed "treasures;" and for being so patient while I spent so much time with my "nose in the books."

Introduction

On April 11, 1612, Edward Wrightman was burned at the stake in Litchfield, England for declaring that the baptism of infants was an abominable custom. His death was the last execution of someone in England for being a Baptist! He had been preceded by countless thousands over hundreds of years.

What would cause so many Christians to be willing to sacrifice their lives for their convictions? What would cause so many kings, governors, rulers, and ecclesiastical bishops to hate those principles and the people who held those convictions so dearly? In the Twentieth Century, the name *Baptist* has been given many meanings; but, historically, Baptists have been evangelical Christians holding to the basic truths of the Christian faith and the following six doctrines:

- The Bible as the sole authority for faith and practice;
- Independent, autonomous churches;
- Regenerated church membership;
- Baptism by immersion of believers only, and the Lord's Supper as the two ordinances of the church;
- Priesthood of all believers and soul liberty; and
- Separation of church and state.

These principles are known as the "Baptist distinctives."

Some people use the term *Baptist* to describe only those who can trace their descent to the Swiss Anabaptists of the Sixteenth Century. In this text we will use the term to describe any who have held to the historic Baptist distinctives. From the beginning of the history of Christianity, there have been those who deviated from the simple Bible truths expressed in the Baptist distinctives. Normally the followers of organized, denominational Christianity have been in the vast majority; however, there have always been those who held to these basic, simple truths.

Those people who held to these simple Bible truths have endured great persecution because these truths threatened the established religious authorities. Our Baptist ancestors have been men and women of great courage and devotion to the Word of God. They were heroes and heroines in every sense of the terms. They deserve our deepest appreciation.

There are some people today who use the term *Baptist* without holding to the historic evangelical Christian faith of the Baptist distinctives. This has created tremendous controversy since the late 1920's among those who carry the name *Baptist*. Certainly we should all be free to practice our own religious faith and express our own doctrinal ideas. However, those who use the name Baptist, while denying the truths for which our Baptist forefathers suffered, do their memory and the term Baptist a great injustice.

For the purposes of this text, a Baptist is one who holds to the great fundamentals of the Christian faith:

- The Trinity: God the Father, Son, and Holy Spirit, three and yet one, all fully God;
- The absolute inspiration, inerrancy, and infallibility of the Holy Scriptures;
- The incarnation, virgin birth, sinless life, death, burial, resurrection, and substitutionary atonement of Jesus Christ;
- The personal salvation of those who put their faith in the gospel of Christ; and
- The reality of the Second Coming, Heaven, and Hell.

Those who hold to these fundamental doctrines, along with the aforementioned "Baptist Distinctives," are considered Baptists.

Chapter 1

Sole Authority of Scripture

❖❖❖

The Baptist Distinctives

- The Bible as the sole authority for faith and practice
- Independent, autonomous churches
- Regenerated church membership
- Baptism by immersion of believers only, and the Lord's Supper as the two ordinances of the church
- Priesthood of all believers and soul liberty
- Separation of church and state.

❖❖❖

The first and most crucially fundamental Baptist distinctive is the doctrine that the Bible is the Christian's sole authority for faith and practice. All other doctrines and Baptist distinctives rest entirely upon the reality of this truth.

First, we will examine what we mean by saying that the Scriptures are authoritative for faith and practice. Historic Baptists believe in the verbal and plenary inspiration of the Old and New Testaments. They believe that the entire Bible is a revelation from God, infallible, inerrant, and is God's written Word to man.

By "verbal inspiration," we mean that the Holy Spirit so guided and controlled the men whom He used to author Scripture that not only the ideas they wrote about, but their very words, came from God. He so directed each individual's choice of words that they are, in reality, His words!

By "plenary inspiration," we mean that the entire Bible is the Word of God. Every part of the Bible is equally inspired and the Scriptures that we have now are all of God's intended revelation. No further revelation is necessary until

Christ returns. It is important to remember that the Bible does not contain the Word of God, but that it is, in fact, the Word of God.

By "infallible," we mean that every guideline given to us by the Scriptures is true and proper. None of God's instructions for us today are mistaken, improper, outmoded, or to be set aside. The Bible is to be completely obeyed because it is the Word of God. By "inerrancy," we mean that God has kept the Scriptures from any error: theological, philosophical, moral, historical, or scientific! Every statement in Scripture can be trusted in its entirety.

There are a number of Scriptures which make clear these basic truths about God's Word.

> "All scripture *is* given by inspiration of God, and *is* profitable for doctrine, for reproof, for correction, for instruction in righteousness: That the man of God may be perfect, throughly furnished unto all good works" (II Timothy 3:16-17).

> "Being born again, not of corruptible seed, but of incorruptible, by the word of God, which liveth and abideth for ever. For all flesh *is* as grass, and all the glory of man as the flower of grass. The grass withereth, and the flower thereof falleth away: But the word of the Lord endureth for ever. And this is the word which by the gospel is preached unto you" (I Peter 1:23-25).

> "Knowing this first, that no prophecy of the scripture is of any private interpretation. For the prophecy came not in old time by the will of man: but holy men of God spake *as they were* moved by the Holy Ghost" (II Peter 1:20-21).

> "Study to shew thyself approved unto God, a workman that needeth not to be ashamed, rightly dividing the word of truth" (II Timothy 2:15).

All orthodox, fundamental Christians agree with the

doctrine previously expressed as to the full inspiration of Scripture. However, historically, Baptists have taken their position on Scripture one important step further. Baptists (and only a very few others) teach that Scripture is the sole authority for faith and practice. Many who hold a view of full inspiration will say that the Bible is the final authority or that it is the ultimate authority. This means that they accept the Bible as inspired, and that nothing may contradict the Scriptures, but that there may be other spiritual authorities on matters upon which the Scripture does not speak. Usually these other possible authorities will be:

- additional revelation from God (e.g., charismatic movement);
- church councils (e.g., orthodox Presbyterians); or
- tradition, church history, or a prominent spiritual teacher (e.g., Roman Catholicism).

However, all of those are unreliable. Historic Baptists teach us that not only is everything in the Bible true, but that everything we need is in the Bible. Baptists do not accept the concept of additional revelation, authoritative decisions by church councils, human tradition, examples of leadership, or history as spiritual authorities. God has given us everything essential to our spiritual well-being in the Scriptures. It is impossible to over-estimate the importance of this one concept — the sole authority of Scripture.

Scripture teaches that God has given us legitimate human authority with certain areas of control over our lives (see Romans 13:1-7 and I Peter 2:13-16). Obedience to human authority (as expressed in its limited legitimate area) is obedience to the will of God as expressed in the Scriptures. Bible examples of human authority include:

- pastors,
- civil government,
- husbands,
- parents, and
- employers.

While their authority is real, and it is Scriptural, it must be remembered that it is also personal and limited.

Parents may express the will of God for their children, but they cannot express it for other families. A pastor may provide legitimate spiritual leadership for his own congregation, but he cannot exercise authority over other congregations. Civil government, while having a God-given role in maintaining law and order, has no place in the spiritual lives of people, the affairs of churches, or in teaching or establishing doctrine.

Obviously, wise men and women will learn from Godly examples; but, however much helpful information we may gain about methods or procedures, these are not infallible spiritual truths and should never be treated as such.

Thoughtful Christians will always be careful in their interpretation of Scripture. Saying that Scripture is our authority, and then saying that there is no way to be sure what it teaches, makes our doctrine of Scripture meaningless.

To be effective in our use of Scripture, we must practice literal interpretation. We must not find fanciful meanings but recognize the normal use of words. We must realize that the issue is not what Scripture means to us; but rather, what the Holy Spirit was saying through the human authors of the Bible. The meaning is contained in the content of Scripture, not in our imagination or personal opinion. The key to proper Scripture interpretation (hermeneutics) is to discover what the authors meant.

The doctrine of sole authority reminds us that our task is to "discover" the truth of Scripture, not to "decide" the truth of Scripture.

The doctrine of sole authority leads directly to the doctrine of separation of church and state. If the Word of God is our only authority for faith and practice, then the state cannot become a spiritual authority over the affairs of the church or the spiritual lives of individual Christians.

Peter and John made this truth clear when they resisted the attempt of the local Jewish rulers to stop their ministry.

"And they called them, and commanded them not to speak at all nor teach in the name of Jesus. But Peter and John answered and said unto them, Whether it be right in the sight of God to hearken unto you more than unto God, judge ye. For we cannot but speak the things which we have seen and heard" (Acts 4:18-20).

Peter and the apostles soon reaffirmed this truth to local rulers.

"And when they had brought them, they set *them* before the council: and the high priest asked them, Saying, Did not we straitly command you that ye should not teach in this name? and, behold, ye have filled Jerusalem with your doctrine, and intend to bring this man's blood upon us. Then Peter and the *other* apostles answered and said, We ought to obey God rather than men" (Acts 5:27-29).

It is this doctrine that has so often led to governmental persecution of Baptists. Throughout history most governments and most governmental leaders have felt that their authority was unlimited. This caused them to constantly interfere in the religious practices and personal lives of the people they ruled. The doctrine of religious liberty is the ultimate enemy of tyranny. Where people are free to believe as their hearts and minds dictate and to practice their religious faith, soon all of the other corresponding freedoms will follow. Monarchs, dictators, and hoodlums throughout history have understood this and have fought the doctrine of religious liberty as though their rule depended on it (and in reality, it did).

As we will see later, Baptists played a major role in establishing the concept of religious liberty as a major factor in the American system of government.

The Bible makes it clear that we cannot get our source of spiritual authority from any other source than the Word of God.

"But in vain they do worship me, teaching *for* doctrines the commandments of men" (Matthew 15:9).

We are clearly taught in Scripture that the state does have a proper place and that we must be careful to properly respond to the state in its area of authority. We are reminded, "Render therefore unto Caesar the things which are Caesar's . . ." (Matthew 22:21a). Again, we are also clearly taught that the role of the state is limited, and we must give unto the Lord that which is His proper due, ". . . and unto God the things that are God's" (Matthew 22:21b).

Chapter 2

Other Baptist Distinctives

"And I say also unto thee, That thou art Peter, and upon this rock I will build my church; and the gates of hell shall not prevail against it" (Matthew 16:18).

The other doctrinal distinctives of the Baptists flow naturally from their basic doctrine —the sole authority of Scripture.

The independent, autonomous church is a doctrine derived from several clear Bible truths. If there can be no other spiritual authority than Scripture, then there can be no group of men who can serve as a spiritual authority for the church. The church is obligated to God's Word.

It is also clear from the Bible that local churches settled their own problems. The principle of congregational church government is seen as the church at Jerusalem elected its own deacons as recorded in Acts 6. It is clear that spiritual authority for the church is the Bible. It is not the responsibility of the church congregation to decide whether or not to obey the Bible.

Each church has an obligation to choose the best policies and leadership for carrying out the commands of Scripture. It is the responsibility of the pastor to supervise (original meaning of the word "bishop") the carrying out of God's commands. The Bible teaches that all spiritual authority is in the Scripture itself, but it also teaches that supervisory authority over the church program is in the hands of the pastor as God tells the pastor to take ". . . the oversight thereof" in the church (I Peter 5:2).

In Hebrews, God commands us to "Remember them

which have the rule over you" (Hebrews 13:7). Again, He tells us to "Obey them that have the rule over you, and submit yourselves" (Hebrews 13:17). He is referring to pastors whom we are to obey. Paul reminds us, "And we beseech you, brethren, to know them which labour among you, and are over you in the Lord" (I Thessalonians 5:12). Luke reminds us to "Take heed therefore unto yourselves, and to all the flock, over the which the Holy Ghost hath made you overseers . . ." (Acts 20:28).

Voluntary fellowship and cooperation were obviously practiced by the churches of the New Testament. This is important if the work of the Lord is to be carried out effectively. The Scriptures mention two offices within the church: pastor (also called bishop and elder) and deacon. Deacons are special servants of the church whose job it is to serve the church (Acts 6 and I Timothy 3:8-13). The responsibility of, qualifications for, and treatment of pastors is given in Acts 20:28; Ephesians 4:11-16; I Thessalonians 5:12-13; I Timothy 3:1-7; I Timothy 5:17-19; Titus 1:6-9; Hebrews 13:7, 16-17; and Galatians 6:6. The concept of a regenerated church membership is one that very few groups, other than Baptists, advocate. The book of Acts makes it clear that those who believed and were baptized were added unto the church: "Then they that gladly received his word were baptized: and the same day there were added unto them about three thousand souls" (Acts 2:41). See also Acts 2:47.

The word *ecclesia* is rendered "church" in the King James Bible and was not a new word coined by Jesus. It was a common word in current use in the Greek language. An *ecclesia* was an assembly of the people. It was most commonly used to describe the gatherings of citizens in the Greek city-states to conduct town business. There was a predescribed condition of membership which all individuals in the assembly had in common: citizenship in the city-state. Christ makes it clear that His *ecclesia* will be built upon Himself as recorded in Matthew 16:18. The precondition for membership in Christ's assembly (*ecclesia*) is

Christ — the common ground is personal salvation.

While it is true that a few passages about the church picture a time in glory when all saints are assembled together, most passages refer to local, visible assemblies that exist on Earth during the Church Age. All passages about the church refer to assembled believers — assembly is the simple meaning of *ecclesia*. Some early English translations of the Bible (prior to the King James Bible in 1611) translated the word *ecclesia* as "assembly."

A New Testament Church is an assembly of baptized believers for the purpose of worship, fellowship, and the carrying out of the Great Commission. The New Testament pattern is that church members are baptized into the church by immersion.

The baptisms by John, the baptism of Jesus by John, and the baptism of the Ethiopian eunuch by Philip all took place where there was enough water for immersion. It would make no sense to go to the trouble to find a river or pool where there was "much water" and then sprinkle or pour a little water on someone's head. This can easily be done with a basin of water as non-Baptist churches prove all the time. In all of the above-mentioned baptisms, each person voluntarily expressed his faith in the death, burial, and resurrection of the Messiah. All but Jesus voluntarily gave witness to their personal conversions.

Scripture teaches that baptism is a picture of the death, burial, and resurrection of Christ (see Romans 6:1-6 and Colossians 2:12). You do not bury someone by sprinkling or pouring some dirt on the head! You bury a person by completely covering the body. The same is true with baptism.

The Greek word for baptism, *baptizo*, was also a commonly used word in the Greek language. It meant "to plunge, dip, or submerge." It always referred to covering with water.

Nowhere in Scripture is the baptism of infants stated or implied. It is impossible for infants to voluntarily express their faith in the death, burial, and resurrection of Christ. It is impossible for infants to give testimony to a conversion that hasn't taken place. Sprinkling, pouring, and the baptism of infants removes from baptism its Biblical purpose: picturing faith in the death, burial, and resurrection of Christ and giving witness of personal conversion.

The Lord's Supper is taught in Scripture as a memorial of Christ's death (broken body and shed blood) and of His second coming as recorded in I Corinthians 11:23-34. This memorial service in no way imparts salvation but is a picture of what makes salvation possible.

The priesthood of all believers is a doctrine that each individual believer may go before the Lord freely as his own representative. We are invited, as brethren in Christ, to enter into the "holiest by the blood of Jesus" (Hebrews 10:19). We are told that we are a "holy priesthood" in I Peter 2:5, and that we may "come boldly unto the throne of grace" (Hebrews 4:16).

Most religions have especially-appointed priests who are supposed to be representatives of the people to God. This was true in Old Testament Israel; however, with the indwelling of the Holy Spirit in the Church Age we each become our own priest. Baptists have led the way in calling attention to the glorious truth of the priesthood of each believer.

The concept of soul liberty is a related truth. This concept is also implied by the sole authority of Scripture. Soul liberty means that we are responsible only to God (as expressed through His Word) for our doctrine, practice, and conscience. Each individual can interpret the Bible for himself. True service for the Lord must be voluntary. This doctrine does not justify lawlessness, worldliness, or loose living. We must answer to God about our obedience to His Word. We must interpret His Word correctly.

This doctrine does mean that we are free from the traditions of men, personal opinions and judgments of others, and coercion from state or religious authorities. Men can legitimately require their own guidelines for involvement in certain programs such as individual church membership, leadership standards, school attendance, etc. These requirements have to do with personal relationships between people and organizations. No one can interject their personal ideas into the relationship between man and God. "But the anointing which ye have received of him abideth in you, and ye need not that any man teach you . . ." (I John 2:27). Further proof is found in Romans 14:5, " . . . Let every man be fully persuaded in his own mind."

Chapter 3

Was the New Testament Church Baptist?

"And as they went on their way, they came unto a certain water: and the eunuch said, See, here is water; what doth hinder me to be baptized? And Philip said, If thou believest with all thine heart, thou mayest. And he answered and said, I believe that Jesus Christ is the Son of God" (Acts 8:36-37).

In the Seventeenth Century in Holland, William of Orange (the Dutch king), hired two scholars to do a study of the churches in Holland. His ideas of separation of church and state and religious freedom had allowed many kinds of churches to operate openly in Holland. The task he gave the two scholars was to study each of the churches in comparison to the New Testament and to determine which of the churches in Holland was most like the New Testament Church. The two scholars were instructed to be completely impartial in their research.

William loosely identified himself with the Reformed Church though he disagreed with their idea of a state church. He naturally expected that this study would show that the Reformed Church was closest to the New Testament. He prepared to publish the study and have it distributed all over Holland. He was greatly surprised when the study revealed that the Baptist churches of Holland were closest to the New Testament! To his credit, he went ahead and had the results distributed to the whole country anyway.

Obviously, it is of great importance to determine if the early churches, as revealed in the Scriptures, held to the same principles that Baptists preach. We will look at each one of the distinctives from the perspective of the New Testament Churches.

The Bible is the Sole Authority for Faith and Practice

Paul wrote epistles to many of the early churches. He, more than any one man, helped to establish churches throughout the modern Mideast and the islands of Greece.

Paul constantly appealed to the churches to be obedient to the Old Testament Scriptures, seeing them in their proper perspective, and to the revelation that came through him and the other Apostles. He never appealed to the human authority of religious leaders, church hierarchy, a denomination, or the state to solve Biblical issues. We will look at several examples.

Paul and Peter at Antioch

Undoubtedly Peter was a great leader in the early church. Peter was also human and prone to mistakes. When Peter, in order to impress representatives from James (apparently the pastor of the church at Jerusalem), seemed to violate the truth of the gospel, Paul publicly disagreed with him as recorded in Galatians 2:14:

> "But when I saw that they walked not uprightly according to the truth of the gospel, I said unto Peter before *them* all, If thou, being a Jew, livest after the manner of Gentiles, and not as do the Jews, why compellest thou the Gentiles to live as do the Jews?"

No matter how important Peter and James were as religious leaders, the truth of Scripture was more important and Paul saw that Peter and James must bend to the Scripture and not the Scripture bending towards them.

The Council of Acts 15

The early church had a great controversy of the relationship between the gospel and the law. Apostles, elders, missionaries, and believing Pharisees from all over gathered at Jerusalem. There was much "disputing" as different ideas were set forth. The issue was not settled by the majority vote of the religious leaders, but by an appeal to the testimony of the Apostles (the basis for New Testament Scriptures) and the Old Testament Scriptures (see Acts 15:13-21).

Paul makes it very clear that he was not impressed by the importance or leadership of those at this conference:

> "But of these who seemed to be somewhat, (whatsoever they were, it maketh no matter to me: God accepteth no man's person:) for they who seemed *to be somewhat* in conference added nothing to me" (Galatians 2:6).

Paul was only impressed by the clearly revealed truths of Scripture.

Paul and the Traditions of Men

Paul makes it clear that the religious traditions that men develop (no matter how good they might be) can never serve as a spiritual authority. Scripture makes it clear that we have no right to make an issue of personal judgment on any matter. The Word is binding on all believers.

> "But why dost thou judge thy brother? or why dost thou set at nought thy brother? for we shall all stand before the judgment seat of Christ" (Romans 14:10).

> "Let us not therefore judge one another anymore" (Romans 14:13).

That is good advice which continues in I Corinthians 4:3:

"But with me it is a very small thing that I should be judged of you, or of man's judgment: yea, I judge not mine own self."

Paul was concerned with God's judgment, not man's. He further warns of men's tradition:

"Beware lest any man spoil you through philosophy and vain deceit, after the tradition of men, after the rudiments of the world, and not after Christ" (Colossians 2:8).

"Let no man therefore judge you in meat, or in drink, or in respect of an holyday, or of the new moon, or of the sabbath *days*" (Colossians 2:16).

Paul makes it clear that not only was Scripture the ultimate and final spiritual authority, it was simply the only spiritual authority. We have no right to judge anyone by our personal opinions or our traditions. The only judge is the teaching of Scripture.

Independent Autonomous Churches

It is clear in the New Testament that each church was independent from all authority and control by other churches.

As unspiritual as the Corinthian church was, Paul had to constantly appeal to them to solve their own problems. There was no regional bishop, denominational hierarchy, or organization of churches to correct the Corinthian problems. As an independent church they had to solve their own difficulties.

When Paul wished to raise money for the poor saints in the Jerusalem church, he had to do so by appealing for contributions. The saints in Jerusalem had suffered persecution from the local authorities. There was no Bible authority over the local churches to order them to help the poor members of the original church. Only their generosity, as appealed to by Paul and others, caused them to give whatever amount they chose.

Even when the Galatian church drifted into heresy there was no outside authority to stop them. Paul begged them not to abandon the truth of the gospel that he had preached to them (see Galatians 1:6-9, 3:1-5). However, if they chose to go into heresy there was no one with the authority to stop them.

Regenerated Church Membership

Every one of Paul's, Peter's, Jude's, John's, and James' appeals to the local churches, and individuals in those churches, is based upon the truth that they are talking to professing Christians. Their encouragement to grow, to be consistent with the gospel, and to be ordered by Christian love would be meaningless if addressed to a church membership partially composed of lost people.

In fact, all of the writers of New Testament epistles warn that unsaved people will try to sneak into the membership and leadership of local churches (see Acts 20:28; II Peter 2:1; I John 2:22-26; I Timothy 4:1-2; Jude 4; and James 2:18). In many churches today, the unsaved don't have to sneak in; they are born into church membership or are welcomed in with open arms. Throughout church history, many good Christian movements have been destroyed by their second generation for failing to heed this principle.

Baptism by Immersion of Believers Only

It is clear that it took a body of water for Philip to baptize the Ethiopian eunuch as recorded in Acts 8:36-38. (Philip didn't use a few drops of water from one of the water flasks they were carrying.) It is also clear from the eunuch's question and Philip's answer that belief was the prerequisite for baptism:

> "And as they went on *their* way, they came unto a certain water: and the eunuch said, See, *here is* water;

what doth hinder me to be baptized? And Philip said,
If thou believest with all thine heart, thou mayest.
And he answered and said, I believe that Jesus Christ
is the Son of God" (Acts 8:36-37).

There is not one single instance of infant baptism, sprinkling, pouring, or the baptism of a lost person in the entire
New Testament! Not one!

Baptism and the Lord's Supper as the Two Ordinances of the Church

In the book of Acts, we find several references to baptism and the Lord's Supper. These are seen as normal and
basic to church life in the New Testament. The epistles of
Paul have several references to baptism and the Lord's Supper. No other church activity is compared to these or is
placed on the same level of importance.

In I Corinthians 11:2 Paul urges the Corinthians to "...
keep the ordinances, as I delivered them to you." We can
learn three important truths from this verse:
- Paul had mentioned all of the ordinances, and baptism and the Lord's Supper are the only ones he had
covered;
- Baptism and the Lord's Supper are **ordinances**
(points of order), not sacraments (means of salvation); and,
- They were supposed to be continued!

Priesthood of All Believers and Soul Liberty

The New Testament is full of instructions to believers
about their personal spiritual life. John wrote the epistles of
II and III John to deal with specific individuals concerning
their personal response to spiritual things. There is not a single example after the cross of anyone being a priest for anyone else. When the veil was rent in the Temple (at Christ's

death), each believer became his own representative before God.

Separation of Church and State

It is abundantly clear in the book of Acts that the New Testament Church was almost always the object of persecution by the state. From the early persecution of the Apostles in Jerusalem, the stoning of Stephen, the persecution led by Saul of Tarsus, to the Apostle Paul's frequent arrests, and, finally, his imprisonment in Rome, Acts is a continual story of persecution.

The New Testament Church refused to disobey the Lord in order to satisfy the state. It is also easy to see that the church had no control over the state.

If your definition of *Baptist* is that Baptists are evangelical Christians who hold to the basic truths of the Christian faith and teach and practice the historic Baptist distinctives, then it is very accurate to say that the New Testament Church was Baptist.

Chapter 4

Were the Early Churches Baptist?

"And that from a child thou hast known the holy scriptures, which are able to make thee wise unto salvation through faith which is in Christ Jesus. All scripture is given by inspiration of God, and is profitable for doctrine, for reproof, for correction, for instruction in righteousness" (2 Timothy 3:15-16).

By the year 100 A.D. Christianity was strongly represented in Asia Minor, Syria, Macedonia, Greece, Rome, and Egypt. By 113 A.D. a Roman Governor was complaining to the Emperor Trajan that Christianity was affecting the temple worship.

Much is known about the early churches through the writings of the "Apostolic Fathers." These were church leaders who were assumed to have been strongly influenced by the Apostles. These leaders include Ignatius of Antioch, Clement of Rome, Polycarp, Barnabas, and Hermas. All of these men wrote between 100 A.D. and 150 A.D. Also important is an early document called *The Teaching of the Twelve Apostles.*

These writings make it clear that many different ideas developed among Christians from the very beginning. They also make it clear that early Christians were united around the ideas of the basic fundamentals of the Christian faith. People who rejected those basic truths were not considered true Christians.

Several Baptist ideas seem common to all of these early writers. The early churches were universally considered to be local assemblies of baptized believers. Membership was gained in those early churches upon a profession of faith followed by baptism by immersion. Churches were obviously separate from the state and were often persecuted by local governments. Individual Christians were usually regarded as priests and appealed to God as individuals.

From the very beginning, there seemed to arise controversy over the Lord's Supper. Some early leaders such as Ignatius taught that partaking of the Lord's Supper was important in achieving salvation. Others, such as Clement and Polycarp taught that the Lord's Supper was simply an act of obedience.

There was also considerable controversy over the sole authority of the Scriptures. Scripture had just become the sole authority for faith and practice. The Apostles (and perhaps those associated with them) had still been receiving revelations, signs, and wonders until approximately 90 A.D. (This is a very rough estimate.) Several of the early church writers (Apostolic Fathers) had seen the sign gifts in connection with the ministry of the Apostles. Polycarp, who as a young man was a helper to the Apostle John, had often seen such sign gifts. The books of the New Testament had all been written, but copies of all of the books were not always available to all of the church leaders. It is certainly easier to understand their confusion in that period than it is to understand such confusion today.

It is obvious that in the early church the terms *bishop*, *pastor*, *elder*, and *presbyter* were virtually identical. They all referred to ordained spiritual leaders in the church congregation. It does appear that the term *bishop* refers only to the pastor with the final responsibility in a local congregation, but the idea of a bishop ruling over several congregations in different areas was unknown to the Apostolic Church Fathers.

It is too much to say that all of the early Apostolic Church Fathers were Baptists, but it is clear that Baptist ideas were present. It is also clear that none of the Baptist distinctives are new ideas, and that they were all present in the early church. While our information is not complete, it is entirely possible that some of the Apostolic Fathers were Baptist. For example, Polycarp does not write about all of the issues that we call the Baptist distinctives, but on each issue that he does write, he is clearly Baptist.

Another important source of information about the early church are the Apologists. These men wrote explanations of Christianity for the heathen world. (Explanation is the original meaning of the word *apology*.) Such men as Justin Martyr, Tatian, Athenagoras, and Theophilus of Antioch wrote during the Second Century to explain Christianity in terms that pagans could understand. While the nature of their work did not cause them to comment on all the areas expressed in the Baptist distinctives, they always relate with the Baptist principle of separation of church and state and often with sole authority of Scripture.

The Apologists had the particularly difficult task of explaining separation of church and state to the tyrants ruling the Roman Empire. They tried to communicate the truth that separation of church and state did not mean that individual Christians were lawless. They also had to explain that this truth did not demand rebellion against Caesar. The early Apologists were unanimous in their defense of separation of church and state. This makes it obvious that this was virtually the universal position of the early Christian churches.

The next important group of writers are the men referred to as the early Church Fathers. They wrote during the late Second Century and the early Third Century. They include Irenaeus (who had been influenced by Polycarp), Tertullian, Cyprian, Clement of Alexandria, and Origen. By this time, professing Christianity was becoming more and more organized and the independence of local churches was fading. The range of ideas held by professing Christians was constantly expanding. However, the controversies of these periods tell us something about the beliefs of the churches just preceding this period.

There was conflict over the idea of infant baptism, and the conflict shows that this was obviously a new idea. It was very difficult for the advocates of infant baptism to convince the churches to abandon their long established position of baptism by immersion of believers only.

Many individuals and churches could not accept the growing control of churches in prominent cities over the rural churches. This was a factor in the Montanist, Donatist, and Novatian movements we will discuss later. This factor led to Tertullian's refusing to identify with the organized church groups. It is clear that local churches were accustomed to being independent. Many churches were not willing to give up their independence for the "advantage" of ecclesiastical union.

The wide variety of doctrines held during this period prove that each individual Christian was free to interpret Scripture for himself. It is clear that Tertullian held Baptist convictions, and Irenaeus appears Baptist on each of the Baptist distinctives that he addresses. Cyprian, Origen, and Clement were definitely not Baptists. There was no state church to tell people how to believe, and the church hierarchy was not yet powerful enough to control doctrinal teachings.

Irenaeus chiefly wrote against the heresy of Gnosticism. He was the pastor of a church in modern day France. He was very distinct on the basic fundamentals of Christianity. He wrote extensively about the sole authority of Scripture. He clearly recognized the Bible as the only source of spiritual authority. He felt that the apostolic gifts were no longer in existence. When he was young he had known older men (including Polycarp) who had seen the gifts exercised in connection with the ministry of the Apostles (John, for example). Irenaeus wrote that it was difficult to describe the apostolic gifts in his day because there was no one living who had personally witnessed them. He attributed their absence to the fact that all of Scripture had been written. His writings clearly marked the sole authority of Scripture as a basic Christian doctrine. He died a martyr's death.

Cyprian, Origen, and Clement originated new traditions in professing Christianity. Their ideas will be discussed in another chapter. It is important to note here that their non-Baptist ideas were viewed as new ideas, and it took a great amount of time for them to be accepted by organized Christian churches. They were never accepted by the majority of independent churches. The Scripture was not usually appealed to as the basis for these new teachings. They were supposed to have their foundation in logic, Greek philosophy, or common practice. The fact that such new ideas had trouble gaining acceptance shows that Christians were used to resting on the authority of the Word of God.

From the very beginning of Christianity, there was much disagreement over its various doctrines. This was seen even in the New Testament. It is also clear that Baptist ideas are seen in the very early stages of Christianity and are in no way recent inventions. Certainly many of the early churches and preachers were Baptist. Certainly these early Baptists were the most consistent followers of the Apostles.

Chapter 5

A History of the Doctrine of Baptism

"*The like figure whereunto even baptism doth also now save us (not the putting away of the filth of the flesh, but the answer of a good conscience toward God,) by the resurrection of Jesus Christ*" (1 Peter 3:21).

Around the Third Century B.C., the idea of baptism became common among many religious groups. It was usually used to signify leaving one religious group and identifying with another religious group. This became a common practice for Gentiles who wished to abandon their pagan religions and identify with the Jews. The Gentiles would be baptized (immersed, according to all historical records) in a public ceremony. Most Jews no longer considered the baptized persons Gentiles and welcomed them as fellow-Jews.

After almost 400 years without a true prophet, God sent John to the Jews. He openly preached repentance and faith in the Messiah, and used baptism as a sign of the reality of this faith in the life of the individual. John became so identified with this practice that he became known as John the Baptist. Obviously, John baptized by immersion because he could only hold baptisms where there was a large quantity of water, as recorded in Mark 1:5, "And there went out unto him all the land of Judaea, and they of Jerusalem, and were all baptized of him in the river of Jordan, confessing their sins." Further proof is found in John 3:23, "And John was also baptizing in Aenon near to Salim, because there was much water there: and they came, and were baptized." Note that "there was much water there." Had John been pouring water on their heads, he would not have needed "much water."

Baptism had already pictured an identification with religious truth and a type of conversion to the religious world. The form of baptism by immersion — plunging someone into the water and bringing them out again — provided a beautiful picture of the death, burial, and resurrection of the promised Messiah. This is important in considering the baptism of Christ. He did not need baptism as a sign of conversion. He was sinless and the Saviour. With His baptism, He did, however, identify Himself with the truth that John was preaching, and He did picture His own death, burial, and resurrection. There is also no doubt that John baptized Jesus by immersion.

> "And it came to pass in those days, that Jesus came from Nazareth of Galilee, and was baptized of John in Jordan. And straightway coming up out of the water, he saw the heavens opened, and the Spirit like a dove descending upon him: And there came a voice from heaven, *saying,* Thou art my beloved Son, in whom I am well pleased" (Mark 1:9-11).

Notice that they came "up out of the water." No pouring took place here!

Baptism of new converts was the clear command of Christ as expressed in the Great Commission in Matthew 28:19. "Go ye therefore, and teach all nations, baptizing them in the name of the Father, the Son, and the Holy Ghost." It was clearly the practice of the New Testament Churches as seen in Acts 2:41, "Then they that gladly received his word were baptized: and the same day there were added *unto them* about three thousand souls." Notice also the baptisms in connection with the conversions of Lydia (Acts 16:15), the Philippian jailer (Acts 16:32), and Stephanas (I Corinthians 1:16).

It was easy for the early church to keep the form of baptism (immersion) clear. As long as Greek was commonly read or spoken, it was easy to remember that true baptism was by immersion. The Greek verb *baptizo* and the nouns *baptisma* and *baptismos* were common words in the Greek language. These words had many uses other than in reference to the religious ceremony of baptism. These words always meant "to dip, plunge, or cover with water." Because of common familiarity with the Greek language, there was little controversy over the form of baptism for hundreds of years except over the compromise of clinic baptism. For over a thousand years, immersion was the standard form of baptism even when infants were baptized. As late as the Sixteenth Century, such famous historical characters as Henry VIII and Elizabeth I were baptized by immersion as infants.

Clinic baptism was the concept of sprinkling those who were physically limited or crippled. The reasoning was that since immersion was difficult for variously handicapped individuals, then God would accept sprinkling as the best that could be done in such cases. This practice began as early as the Second Century A.D. This unfortunate compromise became extremely important after familiarity with the Greek language ceased. Many who no longer understood the background of the word *baptism* assumed that any identification with Christ, as signified by water, was Bible baptism.

Unfortunately, the early churches did not find it as easy to keep the doctrine of baptism as clear as they did the mode of baptism. As early as the Third Century, a church leader named Cyprian, the bishop of Carthage, taught that baptism, the Lord's Supper, and identification with the church were essential for conversion. This is the first clear example of the teaching of baptismal regeneration. While Cyprian did not use this teaching to justify the baptism of infants, others soon did. Apparently others had already conceived of the idea of infant baptism because Tertullian strongly taught against the idea in the Third Century.

As Emperor Constantine began to merge the church and the state in the Fourth Century, baptism took on a new meaning to many people. Baptism was now looked upon as a sign of homage to the state and was often associated with citizenship. When Justinian, in 550 A.D., ordered all non-Christians in the Roman Empire to become Christians, he ordered them all, including the children, to be baptized. Later, in the Ninth Century, when Charlemagne ordered whole Germanic tribes to become Christians, he forced everyone to be baptized, including the infants. Refusal to practice infant baptism became a sign of political resistance.

Many individuals and groups refused to go along with the union of church and state and the concept of infant baptism. At times, local leaders would tolerate such nonconformity, but often these separatists were bitterly persecuted. It is impossible to estimate how many millions have been put to death for refusing to go along with the related ideas of infant baptism and the union of church and state. We will study many such groups and individuals.

Infant baptism by immersion as a sign of church membership and citizenship became the normal teaching about baptism. As the Roman Catholic system grew in strength, power, and organization, the idea of baptism as a part of salvation became more and more common. It was by denial of these doctrines that non-conformity to the Roman Catholic Church was usually identified.

The difficulties of baptizing infants by immersion gradually led the Roman Catholic leadership to adopt baptism by sprinkling. This did not become common until the Twelfth Century, and it was still not accepted in many countries until the Seventeenth Century.

The Protestant reformers brought a whole new discussion of baptism to the religious world. The Protestants rejected those teaching Baptist ideas (sometimes even putting them to death). They did, however, teach the glorious truth of salvation by faith. This teaching was incompatible with the Roman Catholic doctrine of baptism.

Most Reformers finally concluded that infant baptism, usually by sprinkling, was good, that it constituted church membership (and sometimes citizenship), but it was not a part of personal conversion. They also baptized adult converts by sprinkling. Many equated sprinkling with the Old Testament rite of circumcision (which created citizenship in Old Testament Israel).

For almost 300 years there were three main teachings about baptism:

● The Roman Catholic teaching of sprinkling infants as a part of their salvation and for church membership;

● The Protestant teaching of baptism (usually by sprinkling) of infants for church membership; and

● The Baptist teaching of baptism by immersion of believers only.

In the Seventeenth Century in England, the Church of England was determined to do away with the practice of baptism by immersion in that nation. The government printed new Greek lexicons (dictionaries of word usage between two languages) which falsely stated that *baptizo* meant "sprinkle." However, there were still many Greek students in England who knew better, and the new lexicons were ridiculed and soon withdrawn from public use.

In the mid-Nineteenth Century, a new teaching became popular. This teaching is usually known as Campbellism. A Baptist named Alexander Campbell, especially active in Kentucky and Tennessee, began to teach that the act of baptism was a part of expressing faith. He clearly taught that you had not really expressed faith or been converted until you had been baptized by immersion in a church which taught this doctrine. This addition to the gospel was rejected by the vast majority of Baptists. Soon the Campbellites formed a separate movement calling themselves "Disciples of Christ" or "Church of Christ." This created a fourth distinct teaching about baptism.

Baptism by immersion as a testimony of saving faith in

Christ should be more than just a doctrine in a textbook. It should be a beautiful experience in your own Christian life.

If you have not been personally born again, you should confess that you are a sinner, and put your faith in Christ's death, burial, and resurrection as payment for your sin.

If you have been saved but have not yet been baptized, you should make arrangements to do so. Baptism is the first proper step of obedience for Christians and gives the new Christian a good conscience before the Lord.

Chapter 6

A Comparison of Baptists with Other Denominations, Cults, and Movements

"But speak thou the things which become sound doctrine" (Titus 2:1).

"That we henceforth be no more children, tossed to and fro, and carried about with every wind of doctrine, by the sleight of men, and cunning craftiness, whereby they lie in wait to deceive; But speaking the truth in love, may grow up into him in all things, which is the head, even Christ" (Ephesians 4:14-15).

The purpose of this study is not to be critical but to clearly discern where different religious groups, movements, and denominations stand on the ideas which we have studied as the Baptist distinctives. Some of the groups we will examine are movements centered around ideas or doctrines that cut across the lines of several denominations. Others are long-established Christian denominations, while still others are more recent, less established groups claiming to be the only true representatives of Christianity.

Modernism

Modernism is a movement which denies the complete inspiration of Scripture, and thus, denies any special role as a spiritual authority for the Bible. Modernists usually deny the deity of Christ, personal salvation, and the basic Christian truths. They may occasionally hold to one or more of the Baptist distinctives, but only because they are impressed with the logic of such a position and not because it is taught in the Bible. Unfortunately, modernism has penetrated many religious movements and is taught under many names. There are even many modernist churches which use the name *Baptist* even though they deny all the basics of Baptist doctrine and history.

Roman Catholicism

Roman Catholicism is the world's largest denomination that is Christian in name.

Roman Catholics claim an unbroken line of church succession back to the Apostle Peter whom they promote as the first Pope. In reality, the modern Roman Catholic structure can only be traced as far back as the Fifth Century (and that is stretching it some). Roman Catholicism is, in many ways, the complete opposite of the Baptist faith.

- Roman Catholicism denies salvation by faith and insists upon salvation by works and penance.
- Roman Catholicism presents church tradition, the authority of the Pope, and church councils as equal with Scripture as spiritual authorities.
- Roman Catholic churches are in no way independent, but under the control of a world-wide ecclesiastical system.
- Since Roman Catholicism does not hold to a belief in personal salvation by faith, they have no concept of a regenerated church membership. A person becomes a member of the Roman Catholic Church by being born into it or by expressing allegiance to the Church.
- Roman Catholics teach baptism by sprinkling of all infants born to Catholics. Most Catholics believe that this baptism plays a role in salvation.
- Roman Catholicism teaches that there are six other ordinances (including communion) and that they all play a role in salvation. Because these activities are believed to influence salvation, Catholics usu-

ally call them "sacraments" instead of ordinances.

- Roman Catholicism teaches that only those ordained by the church can be considered priests and that others must approach the Lord through these ordained priests.

- Roman Catholicism does not teach soul liberty, teaching instead that only the church can interpret Scripture. In the past (and still in some parts of the world), Roman Catholicism has opposed the idea of individual Catholics owning Bibles.

- Throughout history, Roman Catholicism has stood as the ultimate opponent of separation of church and state. The bloody history of western civilization, from the Sixth Century through the Eighteenth Century, is basically the story of Catholic struggle for control of individual governments. Even today, Roman Catholicism has a tremendous impact on the governments of several countries.

Presbyterianism

This movement is sometimes referred to as "Calvinism" or the "Reformed" movement. Many churches which carry the name *Presbyterian* have been influenced by modernists; however, there is a substantial minority which still hold to the basic tenets of historic Presbyterianism. The original Presbyterian churches taught the same basic fundamentals of the Christian faith as the Baptists. There are many examples of historic Presbyterians and historic Baptists working together to share the gospel with the world (especially in the United States). However, historic Presbyterians have taken an entirely different approach to most of the truths expressed as the Baptist distinctives.

- Historic Presbyterianism teaches that the Bible is the *final* authority for faith and practice, but they place great emphasis on the role of the church in interpreting the Word of God.

- Historically, Presbyterian churches are under the

control of a denominational hierarchy. However, in recent years in the United States, more and more Presbyterian churches are independent congregations.

- Most Presbyterian churches allow for the idea of children being born as church members. Their strong belief in covenant theology (predestination) convinces them that those children are predestinated to salvation. In reality, this often allows unconverted adults to influence a church of which they became members at birth.

- Most Presbyterians accept immersion, sprinkling, or pouring as equally acceptable methods of baptism. Some Presbyterian groups only accept one method, usually sprinkling.

- Presbyterians usually accept baptism and the Lord's Supper as the only two ordinances.

- In theory, Presbyterians accept the priesthood of all believers and the concept of soul liberty. In practice, however, their great emphasis on decisions made by the presbytery (local groupings of pastors) makes it difficult to live by these truths.

- Historic Presbyterians have strongly taught the idea of a church-dominated state. In the early decades of the Presbyterian movement (Sixteenth and Seventeenth Centuries), this often caused them to persecute and violently oppose Baptists. In more recent history in America, many Bible-believing Presbyterians have taught a more moderate form of union of church and state, and many born-again Presbyterians have formed into Bible-believing churches and have even formed their own fundamental Presbyterian denominations.

Methodism

Methodism was founded as a result of the revivalistic preaching of John Wesley in England in the 1700's. Wesley was used of God to call many people to a respect for the Scriptures and the concept of personal salvation. Bible-believing Methodists and Baptists often worked together to take the gospel to a needy world.

Methodism was based upon the basic fundamentals of the evangelical Christian faith and union together in a church system. Methodist churches and individuals were left to decide many things for themselves. Most of them accepted the Bible as the final authority for faith and practice. (They could not accept it as the *sole* authority because they also had the authority of their church system.) Methodist churches have always been allowed more independence than most churches in a denominational system, but the final church authority still remains with the denomination. Most Methodist churches baptize infants and admit them to church membership. Most of their churches practiced immersion, sprinkling, and pouring, leaving the choice to the individual. A few Methodists have been known for holding to baptism by immersion of believers only. Historic Methodists usually hold to only two church ordinances: baptism and the Lord's Supper.

Methodists have historically held to soul liberty, the priesthood of all believers, and separation of church and state.

Today, many Methodist churches are dominated by modernists. Some of the more evangelical groups in the historic Methodist tradition are the Free Methodists, Wesleyans, Bible Methodists, Nazarenes, and Pilgrim Holiness. Most historic Methodists hold to Arminian doctrine (the belief that you can lose your salvation).

Pentecostalism

Also known as the charismatic or tongues movement, Pentecostalism has been an important force in evangelical Christianity during the Twentieth Century. Pentecostals believe that they still manifest the apostolic gifts today.

Pentecostals disagree on many points (including the

—45—

ones that we call the Baptist distinctives). No Pentecostal group, however, can hold to the idea of sole authority of Scripture for faith and practice because they believe that they still receive supernatural revelations from God. You will find Pentecostals who agree with Baptists on each of the other Baptist distinctives as well as finding those who disagree. The Assemblies of God denomination, for example, holds to a regenerated church membership, baptism by immersion of believers only and the Lord's Supper as the two ordinances, the priesthood of all believers, soul liberty, and separation of church and state. They put limits on the independence of the local church and believe in additional revelation.

Traditionalist Protestant Groups

Such groups as the Lutherans, Episcopalians, and Anglicans came out of the background of the Reformation in Europe. They all have the influence of evangelical truth in their background. Historically, however, their emphasis on church tradition has kept them from agreeing with any of the Baptist distinctives. Denominational church structure, infant baptism, sprinkling, union of church and state, and the concept of a restricted priesthood (clergy) are common to all three groups. All three groups are heavily influenced by modernism and are theologically corrupt.

Pseudo-Christian Cults

Many groups have originated in America which claim to be the only true expression of Christianity. Some examples include the Mormons, Jehovah's Witnesses, Seventh Day Adventists, The Way, Unification (Moonies), Christian Science, and Unity. These groups all deny the true deity and Messiahship of Jesus Christ and salvation by faith in His death, burial, and resurrection. Consequently, there is no common ground between those groups and historic Baptists — none!

Because those movements use the Bible, they will occasionally teach one of the truths that Baptists emphasize. Some examples would include the Mormons on baptism by immersion and priesthood of all believers, and Jehovah's Witnesses on separation of church and state. However, there has never been any basis for fellowship or mutual recognition between these groups and Baptists because they take entirely different approaches toward Christian truth.

Chapter 7

Persecution of the Early Church

"And to him they agreed: and when they had called the apostles, and beaten them, they commanded that they should not speak in the name of Jesus, and let them go. And they departed from the presence of the council, rejoicing that they were counted worthy to suffer shame for his name. And daily in the temple, and in every house, they ceased not to teach and preach Jesus Christ" (Acts 5:40-42).

The first 300 years of church history are usually called the Heroic Age of the Church. Christ had forewarned His disciples that they would be persecuted as He was persecuted. This is seen everywhere in the first 300 years of the Christian Era.

The leaders of the Jewish Sanhedrin began the first persecution of Christians. They killed Stephen. Herod killed James in order to please the Jewish leaders; then, they imprisoned Peter and harassed the entire church. Under a leader named Saul of Tarsus, they viciously persecuted the entire church in Jerusalem, beating, imprisoning, and killing the members of that first church. After Saul was converted, he became the great missionary leader, Paul. All through his ministry he was persecuted by the Jewish leaders.

The first official Roman persecution came in 64 A.D. during the reign of Emperor Nero. Most of Rome had been devastated by a fire which had burned out of control. Many people believed, with good reason, that Nero had ordered the fire started to destroy his political opposition. Nero needed a scapegoat to divert attention from himself, and the Christians seemed to be a logical choice.

The Christians, while having attracted thousands to their churches, were still a very small and unpopular minority in Rome. Nero blamed them for the fire and unleashed a vicious persecution against them. Many Christians were crucified while others were thrown to wild animals. Still others were covered with pitch and burned on stakes in the gardens surrounding the imperial palace. In the evening, Nero walked through his gardens that were illuminated by the burning bodies of Christians! According to early church tradition, both Paul and Peter were executed during this persecution that extended throughout the city of Rome.

For the next 100 years, there was no persecution from the imperial government; however, persecutions were common in some local regions, and many Christian leaders were put to death, including Ignatius, Polycarp, Justin Martyr, Irenaeus, and Cyprian.

The Emperor, Marcus Aurelius (161-180 A.D.), decreed that the property of Christians would be given to those who identified these Christians to the government. Throughout the Roman Empire, Christians were reported to the authorities by their neighbors. Many were beheaded, and thousands more were thrown to wild animals to provide entertainment for thousands of spectators who flocked to the Roman amphitheaters. Many times their bodies were burned, and their ashes thrown to the wind or into rivers. Somehow the Roman leaders thought that this would prevent their resurrection from ever taking place!

The Romans gave several reasons for their vicious persecution of the Christians.

- First, they did not understand the almost universal Christian conception of separation of church and state.

Rome demanded that all religions be licensed by the state and that all religions accept the Roman government and Caesar as the final authority. Christians could not, in good conscience, do that. Church and state were separate institutions, and their sole authority was the will of Christ as expressed through the Scriptures. It is interesting to note that principles now known as Baptist distinctives, such as sole authority of Scripture, independent autonomous churches, and separation of church and state, were so widespread and important to the early church. Even evangelical churches in this day debate the reality of these truths! If these truths had not been clear and important to the early church, they could have avoided much of the persecution they endured.

- Christians were also accused of being atheists.

While this charge seems especially ridiculous, we must remember the Romans were used to worshipping idols and people that they could see. They could not see the object of the worship of the Christians, so they mistakenly assumed that Christians did not worship at all!

- Christians were also accused of cannibalism, a charge that came from a misunderstanding of the Lord's Supper.

The vile minds of the Romans caused them to assume that the "eating and drinking" of the Lord's body must imply cannibalism practiced in connection with ritual sacrifices.

Emperor Decius (249-251 A.D.) ordered widespread persecution of all who would not worship the Roman gods and Emperor. Seven years later, another Roman Emperor ordered the deaths of all Christians! Church buildings were destroyed, books burned, thousands of Christians were killed, and many went into hiding. Those were the famous days of the Christians hiding in the catacombs of Rome. There were over 500 miles of tunnels dug in the soft stone under the city of Rome that formed an incredible maze under the city. The tunnels were primarily dug as burial places for the dead, and here many Christians hid and developed their own society. The phrase "underground culture" was first used to describe the existence of the Christians in the catacombs during this time.

The worst persecution, however, was still to come. Diocletian devoted the full resources of the military to hunt down and destroy the Christians. It is estimated that millions of Christians died during that period! That persecution was condemned by Diocletian's successor, Galerius, but that did not return life to the innocent dead. For ten years, every Christian father in the empire had to live with the daily concern that he and his family could be taken and executed by the military.

Fleeing from persecution caused Christians to spread throughout the farthest corners of the empire and beyond. Without a doubt, the message of the gospel was widely spread because of the great persecutions that came to the churches. Remote villages and mountain tribes who might otherwise have never heard the gospel came in contact with devout Christians. Only eternity will reveal how many were reached for Christ as a result of the persecutions.

The ability of so many Christians to remain faithful under the various waves of persecution that they faced also made an impact on the Roman population. It was obvious that these people had something real and sustaining — an inner spiritual strength that other people in the Roman Empire did not have. The number of Christians in the empire continued to grow despite the massive persecutions. Some historians believe that the number of Christian converts in the military was the greatest single reason that the active persecution of Christians ceased.

The depth of conviction maintained by the early churches should teach something to us today. They refused to allow the level of their Christianity to be determined by what was going on in the society around them.

Shortly before the end of his life, Galerius ordered the end of the persecution of Christians, and he was succeeded by Constantine who carried out his desires. Constantine officially adopted Christianity as the religion of the empire; however, there is no evidence that he was personally converted. He began to mix the teachings of Christianity with the religious ideas of several other religions that had a significant number of followers. Constantine was the ultimate politician, offering something for everybody.

Christians were now faced with a new set of decisions to make. There seemed to be freedom from persecution, unlimited opportunity to preach, a great opportunity to influence society with Christian values, and the only doctrines they had to surrender right away were separation of church and state and the concept of the independent church. Right away, two approaches to Christianity developed:

- those that accepted the concept of a governmentally established Christian church and
- those who stood for maintaining the purity of the New Testament church.

Those accepting the established church now seemed free from persecution (though Emperor Julian did try to re-establish paganism by force). Independent (often called "separatist," "purist," or "baptized") churches still had to face persecution. The only difference was that now their persecution came in the name of the Lord! Many Christians chose the apparent safety of the established church.

The Christians were worn out by decades of violent persecution. Many had lost close relatives to the terrors of the Roman persecutions. It is easy to see how they were tempted to compromise. This mistake, however, was tragic. As soon as the government became an authority, the Bible stopped being the sole authority. This opened the door to all kinds of doctrinal change. As the years went by, the established church took a position against every one of the Baptist distinctives.

While Constantine worked at revamping the Christian

religion, he at least tolerated the separatists. They were taxed for the support of the established church, but they were not violently persecuted. Many of his successors, however, took the same attitude toward the independents as past pagan Roman Emperors had against the whole Christian faith.

Theodosius the Great (385-395 A.D.) ordered all inhabitants of the Roman Empire to belong to the established church! He officially sanctioned the growing system of organizational control over local churches.

In 385 A.D., for the first time in modern-day Spain, independent preachers were executed in the name of the "one true church." This was the first such instance — but by no means the last.

Emperor Justinian, 527 to 565 A.D., was the first to order infant baptism. By now, the empire had lost control over western Europe but still maintained control over Greece, the Balkans, and the Mideast. There had been many local persecutions of those people with Baptist beliefs, but now infant baptism was imperial law. This led to the bloody persecution of the Paulicians (see Chapter 10).

It is often hard for Americans to take seriously what our forefathers in the Christian faith suffered. We have been so protected by our system of government that we often take religious freedom for granted. We should be so thankful that we do not have to endure what so many of our ancestors went through. This should cause us to be ever vigilant for the cause of religious liberty.

Chapter 8

Good and Bad Developments in the Early Church

"Remember the word that I said unto you, The servant is not greater than his lord. If they have persecuted me, they will also persecute you; if they have kept my saying, they will keep yours also. But all these things will they do unto you for my name's sake, because they know not him that sent me" (John 15:20-21).

As the early churches were faced with the challenge of being incorporated into the established government, they were faced with many controversies. The results of those controversies have influenced "established Christianity" all the way to the present. The decisions that resulted from the controversies are affecting Baptists and other independent churches to this very hour.

The organized churches met these challenges with different degrees of faithfulness to God's Word. At times, bold, sacrificial stands were taken for certain Biblical truths. Far too often, doctrinal compromises were made. The state church became a mixed bag: standing for the truth in some areas and compromising Bible doctrine in other areas. At times, some state church leaders would stand out for their attempts to be faithful to God's Word within the confines of the state church. Others would totally reject Biblical truth and openly attempt to subject the church to pagan ideas, political concerns, or humanism. We will look at some of the great issues with which the early church dealt.

Apostles' Creed

The first official creed of the Christian church was known as the "Apostles' Creed." It supposedly reflected the faith of the Apostles, and the most common version is as follows:

> I believe in God the Father Almighty and in Jesus Christ, His only Son, our Lord; Who was born by the Holy Ghost of the Virgin Mary; Who was crucified under Pontius Pilate and was buried; The third day he rose from the dead; He ascended into heaven and sitteth on the right hand of the Father; From thence he shall come to judge the quick and the dead; And in the Holy Ghost; The Holy Church; The forgiveness of sins; The resurrection of the body.

With this creed the independent, Baptist churches could agree with one very important exception. The line, "The Holy Church," was interpreted by most people to refer to the establishment of all local congregations into one church organization united with the empire. This, of course, was in direct contrast to the concept of independent churches and separation of church and state.

Arius vs. Athanasius: The Council at Nicaea

Arius, a preacher in Alexandria, Egypt, became the most famous advocate of the idea that Christ was not fully God but was rather a special creation of God. A large group followed him, and he was expelled from the church in Alexandria.

Emperor Constantine did not want the newly united church divided by this doctrinal controversy. He called for a meeting of church leaders at Nicaea in 325 A.D., and almost 300 preachers gathered. Their expenses were paid entirely by the government! Constantine officially presided over their meeting. The union of church and state was coming closer and closer.

The leading spokesman for a clear, Biblical view of the

deity of Christ was Athanasius. He fought for a faithful stand for the Trinity and other basic Christian doctrines. The leading spokesman for compromise was Eusebius of Caesarea. He wanted to create a loosely worded statement that would allow both the followers of Arius and Athanasius to stay within the established organized church. The Nicene Creed issued by this council was a victory for Athanasius and Bible doctrine.

This victory was to be short-lived, however. For 60 years, the followers of Arius and Athanasius struggled for control of the church. The political control of the church organization was proving to be more important than the doctrinal statements of the established church. Athanasius was sent into exile four times (three times relating to this controversy, once by Julian the Apostate) before his Biblical view became established church doctrine.

Council of Constantinople

In 381 A.D., the Council of Constantinople was called to settle a similar controversy over the Holy Spirit. Some taught that the Holy Spirit was an impersonal force, others said that the Holy Spirit was a special creation of God the Father. Others held to the Biblical view of the deity of the Holy Spirit and the eternal Godhead of the Trinity.

After much debate, controversy, and political maneuvering, this Council finally took a clear position for the deity of the Holy Spirit and the Trinity.

Independent, Baptist churches could, of course, agree with the conclusions of the Council of Nicaea and Constantinople. They could not agree, however, with this method for establishing the official doctrine of the church. This procedure conflicted with their doctrine of separation of church and state, sole authority of the Bible, independent churches, and the priesthood of all believers. Ironically, after their defeat at the church councils, many heretics began to champion the cause of separation of church and state and began to form independent churches! It is not always easy to keep the record of the independent, Baptist churches separate from the history of the independent, heretical churches.

Paganism and Ceremony

As time went on, it became more and more difficult to separate pagan ideas and traditions and the ceremonies of the established church. When so many pagans identified with the church (under Constantine and his followers), they brought their corrupt ideas, traditions, and ceremonies, causing great confusion. While several church councils officially condemned paganism, the Roman Emperors introduced more and more pagan ideas into the church. Especially in the official church's ceremonies and rituals, paganism seemed to triumph over Christian tradition.

This, of course, simply confirmed to the independent, Baptist churches their need to remain separate from the organized denominational church system.

Nestorius and the Council at Ephesus

In the Fifth Century, Nestorius, leader of the organized church at Constantinople, began to advocate the ideas that we call *humanism* today. He distinguished between Christ as God and Jesus as man. He promoted a very man-centered approach to establishing religious truth. A council was called at Ephesus to deal with his teaching.

This council clearly condemned both the theological doctrine of Nestorius and his humanistic ideas. This council also rejected the idea of works salvation and human perfectibility taught by Pelagius, a monk and theologian.

Again, these conclusions were agreed with by the independent, Baptist churches because they were in line with Bible truth. However, they were usually opposed by the independent heretical churches.

Augustine

The very prominent preacher, Augustine, a bishop from northern Africa, greatly left his mark on the church during this time. His account of his conversion from paganism and his personal growth as a Christian, *Confessions of Augustine*, has long been regarded as a Christian classic. His preaching and teaching made an important impact on the established church, and his theological ideas still influence many today.

Augustine became, perhaps, the most influential Christian advocate of the union of church and state. His book, *The City of God*, promoted the union of church and state and became one of the most influential books in the history of the world. As the governmental control of the Roman Empire crumbled, the inhabitants of the western half of the Empire had a tremendous opportunity to regain religious freedom and the separation of church and state. However, Augustine's book and his teaching influenced many to look to the church as the new source of government in the west. The state-dominated church would be replaced by church-dominated states!

Augustine vigorously opposed the independent churches. Toward the end of his life, he advocated torture and death as methods to bring the independents into line. He is a hero to many Protestants today, but it goes without saying that he was by no means a hero to the Baptist churches of his time. He also taught the doctrinal ideas of election, predestination, limited atonement, and irresistible grace that later became associated with John Calvin. Augustine taught that any man who rejected infant baptism was an infidel! He believed that the eternal decrees of God were modified when a Catholic priest sprinkled a baby, and baptism would take away original sin! Unbaptized babies were accursed, according to Augustine. That is, of course, pure heresy.

Monasticism

Monasteries became an important part of the established church. Preachers (now becoming known as priests) began to organize in formal communities and withdrew from the day-to-day life of society. Sometimes these groups devoted themselves to social work, sometimes to study. The monasteries did a great deal to foster the idea of unmarried preachers (priests). The very best and the very worst of the established church system can be found in the study of the monasteries. Baptist independents rejected the monastery movement because they correctly feared that this would lead to a separate category of religious leaders recognized as priests. This denied the priesthood of all believers. Under this system, men began more and more to look to other men to represent them to God. Under this approach, the very important doctrine of personal salvation faded and was replaced by a teaching of salvation through the church.

Church Organization

Organization between local churches began before the union of church and state under Constantine. The concept of a bishop (senior pastor) was soon corrupted into the concept of a leader ruling over several churches in one geographical area. This approach was gradually turned into a form for uniting all churches (involved in the church-state system) into one organized church.

When Constantine gave the influence of the Roman Empire to this system, it quickly became dominant, and the organizational structure of the church system quickly included all regions within the Roman Empire. The Emperor became the head of the church system, and, since he was already head of a pagan religion, these two roles quickly became confused. Because of his relationship with the Roman Emperor, the bishop at Rome soon became the most important preacher in the empire.

Roman Emperors soon began to use the title, *Pontifex Maximus*, as the head of the established Christian church, the same that they had used as the leader of a pagan religion. This was shortened to Pontiff or Pope (meaning "Holy Father"). When the Roman Empire crumbled and there was no Emperor in the west, the bishops of Rome gradually assumed the powers and role of the Pontiff. This development created the modern Roman Catholic religious system and denomination.

Independent, Baptist churches opposed this entire process as contrary to the doctrine of separation of church and state.

Chapter 9

Montanists, Donatists, and Novatians

"But and if ye suffer for righteousness' sake, happy are ye: and be not afraid of their terror, neither be troubled; For it is better, if the will of God be so, that ye suffer for well doing, than for evil doing" (1 Peter 3:14, 17).

From the very beginning there were those who refused to accept the concept of the church as one all-encompassing organization. Some were very sincere Bible-believers, others were blatant heretics. Their one common teaching was their claim of independence for the local church.

Montanists

One of the earliest protests against the growing denominational character of the church came from Montanus, a preacher in Phrygia, around 150 A.D. He emphasized the local church and separation of church and state, and opposed the rise of bishops who had control over several churches. He held to all of the Baptist distinctives but one. He believed in continuing Holy Spirit revelation (much like the Pentecostals of our own day), and could thus not be considered an advocate of the Scriptures as the sole authority for faith and practice.

Montanus, however, influenced many churches to act and think independently and to study the Scriptures for themselves. These churches were usually called Montanists, regardless of what doctrinal conclusions they reached. The Council of Constantinople in 381 A.D. declared that Montanists should be considered pagans. In spite of opposition from denominational Christianity, the Montanists continued to grow for several hundred years.

Because Montanists were free to study the Bible for themselves, they often came to very different conclusions. While many of the Montanists would be classified as heretics if they lived today and others would be similar to the modern Protestant movements, many of them held to the Baptist distinctives. It is very fair to say that many of the early Montanists were, in fact, Baptists.

Perhaps the most famous of all the Montanist teachers was Tertullian. He preached in northern Africa during the Third Century. He is often remembered as one of the greatest of the early church fathers, in spite of the fact that he was not connected with the organized church. He is sometimes called the "Father of Latin Theology."

Tertullian spoke out boldly for independent churches, baptism by immersion of believers only, separation of church and state, and the sole authority of the Scriptures. He is sometimes falsely accused of teaching baptismal regeneration, but his own writings on grace make it clear that this is a false charge. He appears to have been genuinely Baptist. He was, in fact, sometimes called "Tertullian the Baptist" because of his strong emphasis on proper baptism.

Donatists

By the Fourth Century, Christianity was becoming strongly denominationalized and was gradually being taken over by the Roman government. Other groups joined the Montanists in separating from organized Christianity. A new wave of independent churches took place in northern Africa. Most of these churches broke fellowship with the established church over the qualifications for bishops, pay from the state for the clergy, purity in the church, and the final authority in solving disputes between the church and state. The movement began to be known by the name of one of its most able leaders, Donatus, pastor of the church at

Carthage.

Emperor Constantine ordered the Donatists to reunite with the recognized church; they refused. He then banished the Donatist pastors and used the army to close their church buildings. He continued to persecute them for five years, but then decided to leave them alone as long as they did not meet in formal church buildings. All through northern Africa, the Donatist churches flourished until they became as popular as the established church.

The Donatist churches tended to develop independently. Normally they taught the sole authority of Scripture, baptism by immersion of believers only, and separation of church and state. Some went even further and taught all of what we would call the Baptist distinctives. They sent missionaries throughout the Roman Empire. They were particularly well-received in the eastern part of the empire where their descendants helped form the Paulician movement that we will study in the next chapter.

Novatians

Perhaps the most important of the early separatist groups to Baptist history are the Novatians. Novatian was an independent preacher in Rome during the Third Century who became so prominent in the western part of the empire that all independent churches were soon called by the name *Novatian*. This term for independent preachers and churches was to stay in use for 200 years.

The normal distinction of Novatian churches was their advocacy of independent churches characterized by the conversion and pure living of their membership. The churches in Rome that followed Novatian claimed to be carrying on the original teachings of the church at Rome. They did not believe that they had taken a new position; rather, they felt that the other churches in Rome had departed from the faith.

Novatian was greatly hated by Cornelius, the bishop of Rome. Cornelius openly criticized Novatian and made so many accusations against him that it is sometimes difficult to sort out the truth from false rumors.

It appears that adherence to what we call the Baptist distinctives was normal for the early Novatians. They were often commonly called "baptized" churches because of their emphasis upon proper baptism. After the first 200 years, their influence all but died out in the west, but they continued to flourish and spread to the eastern part of the empire. Montanists, Novatians, and Donatists often came in contact with each other, and there are many examples of their mutual cooperation. They often accepted each others' baptism as valid. A preacher ordained in one of these churches was often accepted in the other independent churches. There are several records of mergers between different congregations as they realized that they stood for the same principles.

Their influence and growth in the eastern part of the empire may account for the fact that the eastern Greek Orthodox Church has always been more Scripturally oriented than the western Roman Catholic Church.

Persecution by the Moslems

Despite different times of bloody persecution, these independent churches flourished throughout the eastern half of the Roman Empire until the conquest of the area by the Moslems.

At first, the Moslems treated the independent churches better than either the Roman or Eastern Catholic Church had; but, gradually the Moslem fanatics gained control of the empire of Islam and they set out to destroy or convert, by force, all non-Moslems. While the details of these persecutions are mostly lost, we do know that most of the independent churches were overcome by fire and sword. Literally hundreds of thousands of non-Moslems were executed during this period.

It is fair to say that these independent churches were the doctrinal descendants of the Apostles and the early New

Testament Church. Sometimes they could trace their direct heritage to the apostolic churches. (It appears that the Novatians could do this.) These churches led directly to churches that we will study. The Paulicians in the east and the Waldenses, Albigenses, and the Lollards in the west are some examples. These independent churches led directly to the Swiss Anabaptists, the German Brethren, and the Dutch and English Baptists. Our modern Baptist churches trace their heritage to these groups.

It is impossible to over-estimate our debt to these early Baptist groups. They kept alive some important teachings that we rejoice in and live by today.

Chapter 10

The Paulicians

" . . . for he [Paul] is a chosen vessel unto me, to bear my name before the Gentiles, and kings, and the children of Israel: For I will show him how great things he must suffer for my name's sake" (Acts 9:15-16).

When historians try to write about the Paulicians they usually try to connect them with one historical character or another named Paul from the Third, Fourth, or Fifth Century. This is unfortunate and poor historical reporting. The Paulicians were called that by their enemies who accused them of only accepting the writings of the Apostle Paul. In truth, they accepted all of the Bible, but they quoted Paul so often — which is easy to understand since he did write most of the New Testament epistles to the churches — that they became strongly identified with him. If you have to be identified with one human being, you could hardly find a better choice!

The Paulician movement is also often accused of heresy about the doctrine of sin (Manichaeans) and the doctrine of Christ (adoptionism). It must be remembered that the Paulician movement lasted about ten centuries. It is true that these two heresies had heavily infiltrated the Paulician movement by the end of its existence, but the Paulicians had been in existence for several hundred years before these heresies became prominent. It is neither fair nor accurate to only evaluate a movement by its beliefs at the end of its existence.

It is relatively easy to be clear about what the Paulicians

believed. One of their doctrinal handbooks, *The Key of Truth*, has survived until our own day. This book clearly declares all of what we call the Baptist distinctives. The Paulicians were clear in warning that the Roman and Greek churches were turning away from many important truths, including baptism of believers only.

According to the records of the Paulicians, the apostolic faith spread from Antioch into Mesopotamia and Persia and especially into the region of the Taurus Mountains (including Mount Ararat, the resting place of Noah's Ark). From this relatively secure base, their ideas were spread over the eastern half of the Roman Empire and the areas of modern-day Iraq and Iran. Nonconformist groups have often been most successful in mountainous regions where there were natural barriers against persecuting armies. Over the centuries, many Paulicians survived vicious persecutions by fleeing to their brethren in these same Taurus Mountains. Many events of the history of the Paulicians are obscure to us today. During some of the periods of their long history we have only the prejudiced report of their enemies for our source of information. We do have factual information about several important events in their history.

About 660 A.D., a young Armenian man named Constantine sheltered a Christian deacon fleeing from persecutors. In return for his kindness, Constantine was given a New Testament. Constantine studied his New Testament and began to see the crucial differences between Roman Catholicism and the apostolic faith. He engaged in numerous public debates with Catholic leaders. He was immediately identified with the Paulicians, and the government of the Byzantine Empire began its first empire-wide persecution of Paulicians. Constantine was stoned to death, and his chief assistant was burned at the stake. Under the leadership of the Empress Theodora (who hated non-conformists of all kinds), over 100,000 Paulicians were killed in just the one province of Armenia alone! Twice that number were slain throughout the rest of the empire. Many Paulicians fled back to the protection of the mountains.

During this period, there were many attempts by the Paulicians to reach the Arabian tribes for Christ. A number of conversions took place, and a generally good relationship developed between the Arabs and the Paulicians. They often protected and aided one another against Catholic persecutions.

The story of one Arab who was a near convert forms one of the most important stories of world history. Mohammed had extensive contact with the Paulicians, and from them he became convinced of monotheism — the existence of one true God. By his own account, when spirits first began to visit him with the information later contained in the Koran, he was afraid they were devils sent by Satan (which they no doubt were). Mohammed's Paulician friends warned him that the true test for spirits was their acknowledgment of Jesus Christ as God (I John 4:1-4). When he applied this test to these spirits, they immediately denied the deity of Christ. Unfortunately, Mohammed chose to believe them anyway, and the false religion of Islam was born. Mohammed and his early successors remained friendly to the Paulicians, protecting them, and granting them complete religious freedom when they were in Arab-controlled regions. It was 300 years after the death of Mohammed before Moslem fanatics began their wars of extermination against the Paulicians.

In the Ninth Century, the Paulicians drove the Byzantine government out of Armenia and established the free state of Teprice. The church was completely separate from the state and freedom of conscience was granted to all. For 150 years, this government existed. It may be the first government ever which gave a written guarantee of religious freedom to its citizens. Paulicians, other non-conformist Christians, Jews, and Moslem Arabs all lived in complete religious freedom. During this time of stability, the Paulicians sent missionaries throughout the Slavic tribes that make up the background of modern eastern Europe.

It is interesting to note that secular and Moslem historians report that the Paulicians were called Baptists and Sabians (an Arab word for rebaptizers). They have been called "Ancient Oriental Baptists" by such historians as Adeney and Gibbon.

Around 950 A.D., Moslem fanatics overran the nation of Teprice, slaughtering many of the inhabitants. In 970 A.D., Byzantine Emperor John Tzimisces offered the surviving Paulicians religious freedom if they would move to northern Greece and protect his interests there. Many Paulicians accepted his offer, and they became an important buffer between the Byzantine Empire and a land invasion by the Germanic tribes of Europe who later invaded the Byzantine Empire during the bloody Crusades. To its credit, the Byzantine Empire (despite its past record of persecution) honored this agreement as long as it maintained control of Greece.

The missionary interests of the Paulicians now turned to western Europe instead of the east. Without a doubt, Paulician missionaries influenced the rise of the independent Albigenses in southern France, the Cathari in northern France, and the Waldenses of northern Italy.

The Paulicians met with fierce opposition from the Roman Catholic Church, but their ideas continued to spread in spite of the opposition. Paulician assemblies were reported as far away from Greece as England and Germany. They spread throughout Italy where they were known as the Paternes. In Bavaria, they were called the Gazari.

In 1025 A.D., Roman Catholic leaders held a synod for the purpose of dealing with the Paulicians. It is clear that, at this time, they were still evangelical Christians and held to what we call the Baptist distinctives. The Roman Catholics condemned a prominent Paulician leader, Gundulphus, because he agreed with the Paulicians' views and ordered his writings burned.

The Paulicians, who remained in northern Greece, became known as the Bogomils (from a Slavic word meaning "beloved of God"). They were continually persecuted, but their assemblies survived in the mountains until the Six-teenth Century. Many of them continued with the same the-ology and doctrine, though others were drawn into heresy. The Bogomils continued to send missionaries to all parts of Europe. There are even records of Bogomil assemblies as far away as Moscow. Their assemblies were so numerous in Bulgaria that people of Baptist ideas throughout Europe were often called Bulgarians.

When discussing the Paulicians, historians also usually discuss the Manichaeans. This group existed from the Third Century until the Fourteenth Century in what had been the eastern half of the Roman Empire. They denied infant bap-tism and fought for separation of church and state. On these grounds, they are sometimes listed with our Baptist forefa-thers; however, the Manichaeans did not hold to all of the basic fundamental doctrines of Christianity. Their move-ment came from an attempt to combine Christianity with the religion of Zoraster. The Paulicians did not consider them true Christians or recognize their baptism.

The Paulicians were wonderfully used of God to keep the New Testament truths that we call the Baptist distinctives alive and before the world. It is interesting to note that historians estimate that the Paulicians influenced more people in Europe and the Mideast than modern Bap-tists do today.

Chapter 11

The Celtic Christians

"But before all these, they shall lay their hands on you, and persecute you, delivering you up to the synagogues, and into prisons, being brought before kings and rulers for my name's sake. And ye shall be betrayed both by parents, and brethren, and kinsfolks, and friends; and some of you shall they cause to be put to death" (Luke 21:12, 16).

When people hear the name *Celtic* today, they immediately think of a very successful basketball team in Boston. Very few people know where the term "Celtic" came from or why it was chosen for a basketball team. The Celtics were the original tribal inhabitants of the British Isles. Later centuries brought Romans, Danes, Germanic Angles and Saxons, and French Normans to Britain.

All of these groups formed the rich background of the modern-day English people; however, the Celtics were the original inhabitants of England. They were known for their war-like ferocity (which is why a modern sports franchise was named for them). The Celtics demonstrated this ferocity when they resisted the attempts of the Roman Empire to conquer them (First Century B.C.), and again when the independent Celtic Christian churches resisted the armed aggression of Roman Catholicism.

There was frequent trade between the British Isles and the rest of Europe during the First Century of Christianity. Christian teachings soon found their way to the British Isles, and they seemed to have flourished there. The spiritist Druid religion which once dominated Celtic society lost its hold on the British people. It still remained an important force, but by 200 A.D., it no longer controlled the British Isles. Tertullian wrote that Christianity had accomplished what the Roman Empire could not — the conquest of the Druids.

Because of their relative isolation from the rest of Europe, the British escaped being influenced by many of the events that controlled affairs in mainland Europe. Only one of the Roman persecutions extended to Britain (that of Diocletian). When other regions were deeply affected by the merger of church and state under Emperor Constantine, the Celtic churches remained independent, but there was very little organization among the churches.

This concept of independent churches is, of course, one of the Baptist distinctives. Because all British churches were independent, each developed its own doctrinal positions. While many viewpoints were represented, what we call the Baptist distinctives were very common among the British churches of the Second through Sixth Centuries. Separation of church and state, baptism by immersion of professing believers, and the concept of independent church congregations seem universal among the early British churches. There does not seem to be any concept of baptismal regeneration, infant baptism, salvation by church membership, or an organized priesthood before their military conquest by Roman Catholicism.

One of the most famous and most touching stories of church history took place during this period. About 385 A.D., in the village of Bannavern, a boy was born whose father, Calpurnius, was a deacon in the independent church there. The boy was named Succat, though he would be remembered in church history as Patrick. Though raised in a Christian home, as a teenager he became very rebellious toward Christian truth. At age 16 he was kidnapped by Irish pirates and sold as a slave to a pagan Irish chief. The boy became the keeper of the swine for this chief. While alone, keeping the swine, he remembered the teaching of his parents, and he put his faith and trust in the death, burial, and resurrection of Jesus Christ. At age 22, he escaped from his master who had been mistreating him and, following his escape, he returned to his family.

After studying and training to become a preacher, Patrick became burdened for the Irish tribe with whom he had lived as a slave. His family and friends tried to dissuade him, but he was determined to go back there as a missionary! He gathered the pagan tribes in fields near the village and preached the gospel to them and saw thousands converted to Christ. He baptized all those converts by immersion, and then formed local churches for them. The son of a tribal chieftain, Benignus, was converted and Patrick trained him as a preacher. Benignus also baptized thousands of converts! Many more churches were formed through their ministries.

Patrick appears to have believed most of the Baptist distinctives; however, there is some question as to whether or not he accepted the Bible as the sole or final authority. He definitely held to all of the others. The later attempt by Roman Catholics to claim "St. Patrick" as one of their representatives was strictly political and has absolutely no basis in historical fact.

A British preacher named Pelagius began to popularize the idea that humans could be saved without regeneration by the Holy Spirit, while Augustine taught that regeneration took place only as predestined by God. History records that the majority of British churches rejected both of these positions. Their own historians record that they believed that man must be regenerated by the Holy Spirit but that all those who believed would receive that regeneration.

In the Fifth Century, two Germanic tribes, the Angles and the Saxons, conquered much of the British Isles, and they greatly persecuted the Christians. Many believers fled to the mountains of Wales and the wilds of Scotland.

In the Sixth Century, in one of the independent Irish churches formed by Patrick, a young man named Columba decided to go as a missionary to Scotland. He was the grandson of a local Irish king. A church was built on a small island known as Iona, and from there missionaries traveled throughout Scotland, and many young men came there to study. They were taught every one of the Baptist distinctives, and they spread these ideas throughout Scotland. Iona became a college for Baptist missionaries. Eventually missionaries traveled from Iona throughout Europe. Unfortunately, their attempts to take the gospel to the Saxon invaders constantly met with failure.

Finally, the Roman Pope, known as Gregory the Great, determined to bring the British Christians under the control of Rome; consequently, representatives of Rome made treaties with the Angles and the Saxons accomplishing that result. A constant struggle then broke out between Roman Catholicism, backed by the Germanic tribes and the Celtics, for control of their previously independent churches. Three church councils were held, and at all three councils the independent churches refused the control of Rome. But the swords of the Saxons accomplished what church councils could not.

The Saxons began to conquer areas they previously had not controlled, and they continually executed independent, Christian preachers and burned or seized independent church buildings. During this time, a Saxon king, Oswald, and his brother, Oswiu, were converted, baptized by immersion, and convinced of the need for a separation of church and state. They, with a few other Saxons, now identified themselves with the Celtic Christians.

Oswald desired to return as a missionary to the Saxons, but he was compelled to become the military leader of the Celtics. He conquered the area of Northumbria and restored the independent churches there. He called for missionaries from Iona. One missionary, Aidan, was especially successful in reaching the Saxons of the area for Christ. After ruling for nine years, Oswald was slain fighting against another of the Germanic tribes which had been sent by the Roman

Catholics to fight against him. He was succeeded by his brother, Oswiu, in the north and another relative, Oswine, in the south. Oswiu determined to rule the entire area and had Oswine assassinated. It is said that Aidan died from a broken heart as he watched all the leaders cut down in death. To solidify his rule and his relations with the other Germanic tribes, Oswiu converted to Roman Catholicism and became the enemy of the independent churches for which he had once fought. Throughout England, Roman Catholicism became dominant.

The Roman Catholic Church then set out to take control of Iona and, thus, of Scotland. They even succeeded in winning over the pastor of the church at Iona, but he was quickly removed by his people. Finally, a Roman Catholic priest named Egbert persuaded the Iona church to unite with Rome. While many independent churches and believers remained faithful, the independent Celtic Christian churches never again became the most dominant religious movement of England.

Clement of Scotland raised boldly the banner of sole authority of Scripture, but he was forced out of Britain and became a missionary to the Franks. He was eventually executed by the Catholics.

In the Ninth Century, Roman Catholicism controlled Britain which was united under one ruler (Alfred the Great) for the first time. The Catholic hierarchy always had more trouble with this region than any other. The ideas of independent churches and religious freedom remained strong among the English. English preachers constantly refused to preach established church doctrine, and English rulers were constantly defying the will of the Pope.

Many of the Celtic Christians were fully Baptist. Baptist ideas were extremely common, and, at certain times, were held by a strong majority of churches. Their heroic stand for religious liberty influenced later generations of Englishmen. The dreams of Oswald were fulfilled centuries later when English colonists established the democratic republic of the United States of America where religious freedom was guaranteed to everyone.

Chapter 12

History of the Doctrine of Separation of Church and State

"And they called them, and commanded them not to speak at all nor teach in the name of Jesus. But Peter and John answered and said unto them, Whether it be right in the sight of God to hearken unto you more than unto God, judge ye. For we cannot but speak the things which we have seen and heard" (Acts 4:18-20).

The doctrine of the separation of church and state was a crucial principle to the early churches. Literally millions of Christians paid with their lives for being faithful to this Biblical truth. This doctrine, more than any other truth, constantly marked the difference between those who upheld Biblical Christianity and those who followed the idea of an established, organized Christianity. Certainly groups other than Baptist have stood for religious liberty, but no other group has been so identified with this cause.

Tertullian wrote:

> *It is a fundamental human right, a privilege of nature, that every man should worship according to his own convictions; one man's religion neither harms nor helps another man. It is assuredly no part of religion to compel religion — to which freewill and not force should lead us — the sacrificial victims even being required of a willing mind.*

The famous apologist, Justin Martyr, also spoke out boldly for religious freedom. One of his pupils, Lactantius, wrote:

> *Religion cannot be imposed by force; the matter must be carried on by word rather than by blows, that the will may be affected. Torture and piety are widely different; nor is it possible for truth to be united with violence, or justice with cruelty. Nothing is so much a matter of free will as religion.*

These early advocates of religious freedom did not go unheard. In 312 A.D., when Constantine adopted Christianity (without accepting Christ), he originally gave notice that complete religious freedom was his goal. His famous Edict of Milan opens by saying, "Perceiving long ago that religious liberty ought not to be denied, but that it ought to be granted to the judgment and desire of each individual to perform his religious duties according to his own choice . . . ."

Whether Constantine ever intended to follow through with this promise of religious liberty is still debated. What is not in debate is that he soon abandoned such an approach and began creating the church-state system.

Advocates of the separation of church and state were no longer presenting their case to pagan Roman Emperors. They were now trying to persuade fellow professing Christians of what had once been considered a basic doctrine of the Christians.

The doctrine of separation of church and state was one of the fundamental issues dividing the Montanists, Donatists, and Novatians from the established church. One Donatist preacher, Petilian, wrote in answer to Augustine:

> *Think you to serve God by killing us with your hand? Ye err if ye poor mortals think this; God has not hangmen for priests. Christ teaches us to bear wrong, not revenge it.*

Another Donatist preacher, Gaudentis, said, "God appointed prophets and fishermen, not princes and soldiers to spread the faith."

The influence of Augustine once and for all sealed the doctrine of the church-state upon denominational Christianity. Mohammed taught religious freedom, but his descendents out-did Augustine in teaching a religious state. The argument between the two groups was over which religion should provide the state government.

The next thousand years is characterized by the struggle of state religions against each other. The Moslems were destined to conquer northern Africa and the Mideast, and be constantly at war with both the Byzantine church state and the Roman Catholic church states. All three movements agreed upon one thing: their religion should be in control of society. They all persecuted independent churches. The Paulicians, for example, suffered at the hands of all three groups.

By 413 A.D., the Roman emperor, Theodosius II, had decreed the death penalty for anyone trying to convert someone from the state church. By 560 A.D., Justinian had declared the death penalty for any in the Eastern Empire who rebaptized a member of the state church. During the Twelfth Century, three different church councils called for the execution of those who defied the state church.

During the Eighth Century, Charlemagne was a very important figure in the struggle over separation of church and state. For 300 years, governments in the former western part of the Roman Empire had been very weak and limited. While they all stood for a union of church and state, they were able to do very little to enforce such ideas. Most people lived their lives with very little influence from any kind of government.

Charlemagne changed all that. He set out to rebuild the Roman Empire and conquered most of western Europe. On Christmas Day, 800 A.D., he was crowned Emperor by the Pope in Rome. Charlemagne brought various tribes and nations under his government. He also forced tens of thousands of pagans to accept Catholic baptism. His armies marched them to nearby rivers and lakes where priests performed mass "baptisms." He required church attendance and tithing. His soldiers ruthlessly crushed independent churches and rooted out non-conformists and those he called heretics.

The historical record shows that few people advocated separation of church and state during that time. This does not mean that truth had no supporters, but it does seem to indicate that they were forced into the mountains and forests. Undoubtedly, the activities of Baptist churches and other non-conformists went on, but in a very limited fashion. After the reign of Charlemagne, his empire broke up and we again see a number of limited, weak, local governments.

While governments were relatively limited, we see the rise of the Albigenses, Petrobrusians, Waldenses, Henricians, and others. Those bold proclaimers of Baptist doctrine drew the attention of millions to the idea of separation of church and state and other Baptist doctrines. One Roman Catholic historian estimated that one-third of the population of Europe identified with independent churches. This proved to be a great threat to the political and religious establishment. It is a very simple step to go from championing religious liberty to standing for liberty in general.

There are examples in history of the advocates of religious liberty trying to establish new governments for the purpose of preserving such liberty:

- The Paulicians' attempt in the state of Teprice;
- The revolt that was led by Arnold of Bresica in Rome (see Chapter 14);
- The Peasants War in Germany of the Sixteenth Century; and
- The American War for Independence in the Eighteenth Century.

Pope Innocent III led the Roman Catholic Church to the apex of its power in the Thirteenth Century. Under his leadership, the church maintained complete control over the nations of Europe. He has been called the most powerful man who ever lived, and maybe he was. Innocent III threatened to condemn to Hell all the citizens of a nation if the ruler of that nation did not obey him! This was called placing a nation under interdict. The pope's power to do this was so widely believed that no king could oppose him. Eighty-five times he threatened kings with interdict, and all eighty-five times they gave in to him! The Pope forced one king to sign the entire nation over to him.

Innocent III was very aware of the independent churches and, at least twice he attended independent church services without those congregations knowing who he was. From his description, at least one of these churches was Baptist. At first, Innocent III ordered numerous missions to preach to the independents. When this was unsuccessful, he ordered all nations to execute all non-conformists and to close all independent churches. He also ordered vicious campaigns against the Jews. He threatened to place any country under interdict which did not destroy its independent churches.

The bloodiest religious persecution Christians had ever seen was the result of this decree. Innocent (what a name!) III was supposed to be a Christian leader, yet he was responsible for even more deaths than the Roman Emperor Diocletian. Not until the rise of Adolf Hitler in the Twentieth Century did a bloodier persecution shake Europe.

Brave individuals still continued to raise a voice for religious freedom, but their cry was to go largely unheeded until the Sixteenth Century. During the early years of the Reformation, the independents often joined hands with the Reformers to overthrow the Catholic state churches. In those early days, most of the Reformers advocated religious freedom. Many of Zwingli's early soldiers were Anabaptists. Even Luther cooperated with the German Anabaptists during his first few years as an outcast from Roman Catholicism. It is easy, however, to be opposed to the idea of a state church when you are not in power. Wherever the power of Romanism was broken, other tyrants soon rose up to take their place. Soon Luther in Germany and Zwingli in Switzerland promoted their own form of state churches, and they attacked those with whom they had once joined in the struggle for religious liberty.

While the Reformation only saw the rise of one state with religious freedom, Holland, the ideas of the independents gained a wide audience. From the Sixteenth Century, there were always strong movements in Europe working for separation of church and state.

The Dutch House of Orange was to provide two great heroes for the movement advocating separation of church and state. In 1572, William of Orange (also known as William the Silent) granted religious freedom to all the Dutch people. This was the first government since the Paulician state of Teprice to guarantee religious freedom to its citizens. His descendent, William III, later became King of England as well as King of Holland, and brought basic religious freedom to the English people.

The concept of religious freedom has gradually taken hold on Europe. Most European countries still have some limitations on freedom of religion, but there is no comparison to the tyranny that was known in Europe a few hundred years ago.

Of course, the story of the United States and its 200-year history is the ultimate example of religious freedom. This story will be told in a later chapter.

Chapter 13

The Dark Ages

"We have also a more sure word of prophecy; whereunto ye do well that ye take heed, as unto a light that shineth in a dark place, until the day dawn, and the day star arise in your hearts" (2 Peter 1:19).

It is difficult for modern Americans to imagine what life was like during the period that we call the Dark Ages of Europe. This period was not of the same length in each part of Europe, but it covers roughly the Sixth through the Fourteenth Centuries.

With the exception of the rule of Charlemagne in the Ninth Century, there was little central government. Most government was based upon contracts of mutual protection. There was very little law. Violence settled most disputes. Literacy was almost non-existent. It is estimated that less than ten percent of all males and less than one percent of all females could read during this period!

For the vast majority of people, the only major activity was the struggle for survival. Obtaining food, clothing, and shelter was a full-time task for most people. Very few people ever traveled very far from the region in which they were born. It has been estimated that the average person during the Dark Ages never met more than 200 people in his lifetime!

Even the established church priests usually could not read. Most of the priests went through their entire lifetime without even seeing a Bible, much less studying one. Religious teaching, while officially Catholic, was usually heavily influenced by the local superstitions and tribal legends.

Roman Catholicism went through drastic changes during this period. There had been a great struggle within the Roman Church between those influenced by the school of Alexandria and those influenced by the school of Antioch. The Alexandrian school emphasized spiritual interpretations of Biblical statements while the school at Antioch taught literal interpretation of Biblical statements. During the Dark Ages, the followers of the school of Alexandria gained complete control over the Roman Catholic Church.

The church became predominantly a political power. A number of the Popes during this period were very open about their lack of traditional Christian doctrines, ethics, and behavior. Astrology, drunkenness, immorality, and homosexuality were all practiced openly by church leaders and even Popes. The Popes sometimes came under the control of different political powers. For a while, the Italian nobles controlled the selection and activities of the Popes. Later, it was the German emperor who exercised control. After that, the French kings took the power. At one point, the Italian nobles made a 12-year-old boy Pope! He later sold the office for a thousand pounds of silver!

The church in the Byzantine Empire officially split with the Roman Catholic Church, each claiming to be the only true representative of God's will on the earth.

Gradually, the Germanic tribes came under the control of the Roman Catholic Church. This made the church dominant over Scandinavia and most of mainland Europe. Russia came under the control of the Eastern Orthodox (Byzantine) Church.

The established church became characterized by its corruption. There was no standard of morality or righteousness expected of its priests. More and more, pagan ideas and fanciful spiritualized interpretations of Scripture became the basis for church doctrine. Many pagan ideas become common teachings such as:

- *purgatory* — defined as a place of penance between Heaven and Hell from which one can escape after payment of money,
- *indulgences* — payment of money or goods to blot out sins, and
- *salvation by baptism.*

The primary effect of the established church on European life became political and financial.

Various attempts were made to reform the church, and even some Popes took their responsibilities seriously making some temporary improvements. Different groups developed within the established church to try and solve specific problems. Monasteries were designed to protect priests from the influence of the world. Some priests took vows of poverty to protect themselves from the influence of money. Gradually, a vow of celibacy became the norm for priests. It was thought that this would protect them from being drawn into moral impurity. However, as it became more and more common for priests not to marry, moral problems became even more of an issue among the established church clergy. Most reform movements brought about limited, temporary improvements, but the general course of things continued.

Some Popes led the Roman Catholic Church to great moments of power. Gregory VII held such great political power that he could make the German emperor wait barefoot in the snow for three days before seeing him. He then made him bow, kiss his feet, and beg forgiveness. However, such political contests were risky. This same emperor later increased his power and drove Gregory from Rome, after which the Pope died in exile, hiding in the mountains. As we have seen, Pope Innocent III brought the Roman Catholic Church to a place of supreme power in Europe. The will of Pope Innocent III was law, and during his rule no one ever successfully defied his power. Later Popes found it difficult to retain that much control.

The Crusades took place during this time for the purpose of driving the Moslems from Palestine and establishing

Christian (Catholic) kingdoms in the land where most Bible events took place. The First Crusade succeeded in driving the Moslems out of areas of Palestine, and kingdoms modeled after the feudal states of Europe were established. These kingdoms lasted several decades, but eventually were overrun by the Moslems again. A number of other Crusades were launched with very little success. Those Crusades were called for by the Roman Catholic Church, often organized by the Popes. Priests and church leaders always accompanied the Crusades. They were up to their collars in thievery, rape, and killings.

The people of Europe were guaranteed that it was God's will for them to conquer Palestine, but after decades of sacrificing tens of thousands of lives and untold financial resources, the people of Europe were very disillusioned. It began to appear that God did not speak through the Roman Church after all. The Crusades led to a tremendous decline in the power of the established church. Nation states began to arise as related tribes were brought under the control of strong rulers who often felt free to defy the Pope. One French king openly had the Pope beaten for criticizing him. Arguments developed over who the true Pope was with different nations recognizing different leaders as the Pope. Soon, the authority of the Pope was based upon his ability to gain the support of several influential kings.

Day-to-day religious observance drastically changed. Rarely did Catholics attend church services or get any formal religious instruction. People still looked to priests to "baptize" infants, serve communion (which was often done in homes), perform marriages, and conduct funerals. The church still had a powerful hold on the people, but they had very little formal training as Catholics.

When a revival of learning did come to Europe, it had very little to do with the churches. Schools began to form in cities and the rate of literacy grew. Education still came from a Catholic perspective, but most of it was only nominally Catholic. When the great teacher, Abelard, began to urge his students to think for themselves, it was to have great consequences. Two of his students began studying the Bible for themselves instead of studying Catholic teaching about the Bible. They became great Baptist leaders — Peter of Bruys and Arnold of Bresica.

These circumstances created great opportunities for independent, Baptist preachers. Through much of the Dark Ages, they traveled and preached freely. Even when local governments tried to stop them, they often had little control outside the largest villages. Multitudes flocked to hear the independent, Baptist preachers preach the Word. Even terrible persecution under Charlemagne and Pope Innocent III could not destroy this movement.

There was a great spiritual hunger that the corrupt established church obviously could not satisfy. The people were not brainwashed in established church doctrine.

We do not have the details of all the great independent, gospel-preaching, Baptist movements of this period. It would be very exciting if we did; however, even the most biased Catholic and secular historians acknowledge the importance of the independent, separatist churches during this period. We will study a number of such groups through the next three chapters.

Chapter 14

Baptist Heroes of the Dark Ages

"For therefore we both labour and suffer reproach, because we trust in the living God, who is the Saviour of all men, specially of those that believe. These things command and teach. Let no man despise thy youth; but be thou an example of the believers, in word, in conversation, in charity, in spirit, in faith, in purity" (1 Timothy 4:10-12).

The little city of Albi in southern France became the center of tremendous religious controversy. It was in Albi that a number of independent churches defied the Roman Catholic establishment. Soon, independent churches throughout France carried the name of the little town of Albi as they became known as *Albigenses*. It was common among these independent churches to baptize believers only, to advocate separation of church and state, the priesthood of believers, and soul liberty. Some of the churches and preachers went even further and taught the sole authority of Scripture. Many of the independent churches called *Albigenses* were legitimate Baptist churches.

Most of these churches claimed to be derived directly from the Apostles, either through the Paulicians or through an earlier French group called the *Cathari*. Many of the most famous of the Cathari were heretics. The Cathari got their name (which meant *purist*) by insisting upon a regenerated membership in their independent churches.

Many of the original Cathari seem to be Baptist, but

their movement was relatively quickly taken over by heretics.

The Waldenses had missionaries in southern France, but they soon joined with the Albigenses. The Albigenses, Paulicians, and Waldenses often were in fellowship with one another and respected each other's baptism and ordination.

The Albigenses developed their own hospitals, schools, and seminaries while Roman Catholicism declined throughout the entire region. The independent groups were condemned by various church councils, and representatives of the established church were sent to persuade them to abandon their independent churches. Finally, Pope Innocent III ordered them destroyed by force. His order was carried out by destruction of entire cities where the Albigenses had strong churches. The Albigenses were the objects of such hatred that the Catholic establishment was willing to kill thousands of faithful Catholics to be sure that all of the Albigenses were slain. This bloody persecution continued for 20 years. Albigenses who survived hid in the forests or mountains or fled to refuge with the Waldenses. It has been said that of all of the persecutions directed at Baptist groups, this was the most cruel.

Around the year 1100 A.D., Peter of Bruys became a prominent independent preacher in France. He clearly advocated all of what we call the Baptist distinctives and suffered for his stand. He was banished from several areas, but he preached for 20 years in Toulouse. In 1126, he was seized by Catholic authorities and burned at the stake. Those influenced by his teachings formed independent churches and were called *Petrobrusians*. They became so popular that special councils of the Roman Catholic leadership were called to decide how to deal with them.

One of Peter's followers was Henry of Lausanne who preached all over France and Switzerland. Entire Roman Catholic congregations left the established church and became independent. Those churches were known as

Henricians. Henry taught the truths that we currently call the Baptist distinctives. He was arrested after being declared a heretic by Catholic leadership and died in an underground prison around 1148 A.D. The Swiss Anabaptists, 400 years later, claimed that their churches sprang from the Henricians and Petrobrusians who fled to the Alps. Swiss Anabaptists were also influenced by the Waldenses.

Arnold of Bresica was a lifelong campaigner for separation of church and state, and his work caused him to be banned from one country after another. He finally moved to Rome where his strong teaching led the people of Rome to overthrow the Pope and drive him from the city. For a time, the people of Rome were free, and many independent churches operated openly. Arnold identified himself with the Baptist distinctives, and soon many of the independent churches were called *Arnoldists*. He gained many followers in the Italian region of Lombardy. For hundreds of years advocates of separation of church and state in Italy were to be called *Lombards*.

Unfortunately, military forces loyal to the Pope retook Rome, and Arnold was captured and hanged. His body was burned, and his ashes were thrown into the Tiber River. Many of his followers were also killed.

The Arnoldists later identified themselves with the Waldenses as did most of the Petrobrusians, Henricians, and surviving Albigenses.

Berengarius was the director of the Catholic schools in Tours. His study of the Scriptures led him to teach baptism by immersion of believers only and that the Lord's Supper was only an ordinance. He was declared a heretic, and he spent the rest of his life in isolation. He had many followers who often formed independent churches. One Catholic writer estimated that the combined membership of those independent churches was over 800,000. Little is known of what happened to that movement.

There were many others who were valiant for the truth during that period. It is reported that in 1146 A.D. the town of Cologne, Germany had many "heretics" in it. They are described by their enemies as holding doctrines that we know as Baptist today.

In 1165 A.D. a church council was held for the purpose of dealing with an unnamed group of "heretics." The description of their teaching clearly identifies them as Baptists.

Many people of Baptist convictions lived in Bohemia. Some believe that they were a branch of the Waldenses (see Chapter 16). They eventually came under the protection of the Prince of Lichtenstein who became one of them and protected them in his kingdom. It is estimated that some 30,000 independent, Baptist people moved under the banner of his protection. They isolated themselves politically from the rest of Europe, and, even today, the modern city-state of Lichtenstein remains independent of any of the nations of Europe.

Often, the brave, independent preachers of the Dark Ages were branded and tried under false names and accusations. Many times they were falsely accused of witchcraft, and the Paulicians, Waldenses, Albigenses, Bogomils, and others were executed when there was no validity to the charges. Some historians suspect that many of the great multitude executed in witchcraft trials were really preachers of the gospel.

The Bohemian Brethren developed as a distinct movement in Germany, and they may have had some connection with the Bohemian believers mentioned previously. Those believers often maintained their membership in Roman Catholic Churches (which rarely assembled). Those Christians formed independent Bible study fellowships and practiced baptism and the Lord's Supper. Each group was independent, and many fellowships developed Baptist convictions. Their most famous spokesman, Peter Cheleicky, recommended baptism by immersion of believers only. Those groups eventually came under persecution and became independent churches.

The Bohemian Brethren seem to have been influenced by the Picards, another group of German Baptists about which we have little information.

In the next two chapters we will study the two largest groups of independent Baptist preachers, the Lollards and Waldenses.

Chapter 15

Pre-Reformation English Baptists

"*Princes have persecuted me without a cause: but my heart standeth in awe of thy word. I rejoice at thy word, as one that findeth great spoil. I hate and abhor lying: but thy law do I love*" (Psalms 119:161-163).

Despite Roman Catholic control in England, brave souls continued to advance spiritual truth there.

During the Thirteenth Century, Robert Grosseteste, an English bishop, declared that Scripture was the sole authority for faith and practice. He was declared a heretic by the Pope. During the Fourteenth Century, the King's chaplain, Thomas Bradwardine, came to a clear understanding of personal salvation. He was converted and began to preach the evangelical faith. Copies of his sermons spread throughout Europe. He was protected by King Edward III. Bradwardine's further study led him to advocate several of the Baptist distinctives.

John Wycliffe, sometimes called the "Morning Star of the Reformation," became the most famous preacher in England. He clearly preached justification by faith, and he renounced infant baptism. He wrote brilliant defenses of the doctrine of the sole authority of Scripture. Even though he was under the protection of powerful English nobles and was made a chaplain by Edward III, he was forced to retire to the countryside for safety.

Wycliffe devoted himself to translating the Scriptures into the English tongue commonly spoken in the Fourteenth

Century (called Middle English today). He was so committed to the sole authority of Scripture, soul liberty, and the priesthood of all believers that he felt everyone must have his own copy of the Scriptures to study. A whole new group of preachers (many of them converted priests) began to travel throughout England proclaiming these truths and preaching directly from Scripture. They often attracted great crowds and were warmly received by the people.

Constant efforts were made by representatives of Catholicism to get Wycliffe to recant and deny the doctrines he was preaching. Once, when he was very ill and thought to be dying, representatives of four Catholic orders came to see him and demanded that he recant his previous teachings. He rose from his sick bed and declared, "I shall not die but live, and again declare the evil deeds of the friars."

Wycliffe spent fifteen years translating the Latin Vulgate Bible into English. (He did not know Greek or Hebrew.) His translation was wildly received. His following grew until one writer who was a contemporary of Wycliffe estimated that he had more followers than the Roman Catholic Church! Many of his followers were street preachers who taught that the Bible, not the Pope, was the final authority. Many also preached that the Pope was not the "Vicar of Christ," but that, in fact, he was the Antichrist.

During the last years of John Wycliffe's life, he devoted himself to the study of theology. He challenged the Roman Catholic teaching about the Lord's Supper and salvation. He identified himself with the Baptist teaching of Berengarius of Tours and began to hint about the teaching of separation of church and state. These teachings went too far for many of the nobles who protected him, and most of them withdrew their support. Some of his closest associates in the ministry broke with him, but rather than hesitate, he now boldly declared for independent churches and separation of church and state. He was ordered to appear before the Pope, but he refused.

Wycliffe had a stroke and died in church in 1384. His

books were ordered to be burned by the Council of Constance, and his body was later dug up and burned.

Walter Lollard, a Dutch Waldensian, came to England during this period and was clearly a Baptist preacher. He soon attracted a great following who were called, along with Wycliffe's followers, *Lollards* or "Bible Men." (Not a bad name to be called!) They were called "Bible Men" because of their emphasis on the Scriptures as the sole authority for faith and practice.

The Lollards petitioned the King and Parliament for an end to the state church and for religious liberty. At this time, they were estimated to be in a slight majority in England.

They were soon the objects of vicious persecution, sponsored by the King and Parliament. In 1401, a preacher known as William Sawtre was burned at the stake for being a "Bible Man." Following Sawtre's execution, other good men, "of whom the world was not worthy" (Hebrews 11:38), went to the flaming stake:

- John Bady,
- Richard Turming,
- John Claydon,
- William Taylor (a priest),
- William White,
- Richard Hovden,
- Richard Wyche,
- Thomas Bangley (another priest), and
- Sir John Oldcastle.

It is these people who should be heroes of youth today!

The first woman to be burned at the stake in England was Joane Broughton, a Lollard, who was burned at Smithfield in 1494. She was bravely followed to the stake by her daughter!

A tower in Lambeth was set aside to imprison Lollards waiting for trial; this tower is still known as Lollards' Tower today.

The power of the Roman Catholic persecutors was so great that in 1413 they pressured King Henry V into putting his old friend John Oldcastle's to death. Oldcastles crime had been that of advocating personal salvation by faith and the sole authority of Scripture.

Lollard preachers went into hiding, and then assemblies were confined to the remote areas of mountains and forests.

In the late Fifteenth Century, William Tyndale was born in England. His parents were members of an independent Lollard (Baptist) church in south Wales. He was personally converted to Christ while studying the Greek New Testament of Erasmus at Oxford University. Tyndale became a great Greek scholar, and was greatly used of God in bringing the Word of God to the English people. His translation of the Greek New Testament into English had an incredible impact upon the country. A century later, the King James Bible translators were careful to keep Tyndale's wording whenever possible.

Tyndale also wrote doctrinal books which show that he took many Baptist positions. He is on record as teaching the independence of local churches, priesthood of all believers, only two offices for the church — pastor and deacon, baptism by immersion of believers only, and sole authority of Scripture. None of his writings contain anything contrary to the Baptist distinctives. Tyndale was joined in his labor by Thomas Bilney who had studied the Greek New Testament of Erasmus and had been converted. John Fryth, another Greek scholar, was led to Christ by Tyndale. The three men became spokesmen for the evangelical faith and sole authority of Scripture in England.

This was a very unstable time in England. In 1401, King Henry IV of England had laws passed that made the death penalty mandatory for anyone who disagreed with the Pope about anything. English sheriffs had to swear they would persecute every Bible believer in England. When a "heretic" was found "guilty," all the church bells would toll and a priest would grab a lighted candle from the altar and scream, "Just as this candle is deprived of its light so let him be deprived of his soul in Hell." Church leaders took the position that killing "heretics" was their major thrust!

While Tyndale increased in popularity, unmolested by the government, others were persecuted. Thomas Man was arrested for teaching the priesthood of all believers and for having led 700 people to Christ. He was condemned and burned at the stake. Most modern Christians (at least in the United States) do not have to worry about being burned at the stake for winning people to Christ.

The Roman Catholic Church began to teach against the reading of the Greek New Testament or the use of any English translations. Seven adults were burned at the stake for teaching their children the Lord's Prayer and the Ten Commandments in English.

Finally, the established church turned its sights on Tyndale, and even his powerful friends could no longer protect him. He fled to Germany to the town of Cologne, long noted for its independent preachers. Here he worked peacefully for a while, but then the printing of his New Testament was banned in that city. He fled to Worms, and his New Testament was printed there. The impact upon England was incredible. The English New Testament was widely read with great joy.

Chapter 16

The Waldenses

"Yea, for thy sake are we killed all the day long; we are counted as sheep for the slaughter"
(Psalms 44:22 and Romans 8:36).
Psalms 44 is traditionally known as the Waldensian Psalm.

The mountains have always been a place of refuge for non-conformists, their natural ruggedness providing security against persecuting armies. The Alps, mountains in central Europe, have offered shelter and protection to more than one group seeking freedom from persecution. One of the most famous groups was the Waldenses.

There is no one point of beginning for the Waldenses. Their activities are most easily recorded from the time of Peter Waldo — from whom they got their name, but they clearly existed before Waldo. Waldo did not begin this movement, but rather he was reached by this movement of independent churches centered in the Alps. The early Waldenses claimed a direct line back to the churches of the Apostolic Period.

Peter Waldo was a rich merchant and leading citizen in Lyons, France in the Twelfth Century. From some of the independent church people in the mountains, he received a copy of the New Testament. He soon contrasted that with the Roman Catholic doctrine he had been hearing. He translated the Scripture into the local language and began to distribute copies. This led to the formation of a study group in his home. Waldo and others trusted Christ as Saviour, and

Waldo (and others) sold their property and gave the proceeds to the poor.

Waldo and his followers began to preach in Lyons and took mission trips to nearby cities. They usually traveled two-by-two after the pattern of the New Testament. They went throughout France, Switzerland, and northern Italy. Those preachers were often called "the Poor Men of Lyons." They were ordered to quit preaching, but they refused. Their Bibles were pitched into the flames, and 80 of their preachers were burned at the stake in Strasbourg. They were driven out into Austria, Swabia, Poland, Bavaria, Bohemia, and other areas. Waldo fled for his life, ending up in Bavaria. His followers were sometimes called Leonists.

The Waldenses were very clear in their stand for the sole authority of Scripture. Their churches were all independent, and each congregation developed its own doctrines. Baptism by immersion of believers only was a very common belief, though it was not universal among the Waldenses. They taught eternal security for the believer and justification by faith alone. In other words, they were Bible-believing Baptists long before Martin Luther was born! It is fair to say that most Waldensian churches and preachers were Baptists, though some identified with the movement were clearly not Baptist.

The Waldenses were especially noted for a purer lifestyle than the inhabitants of the regions where they lived. Even their staunchest enemies acknowledged their Godly personal behavior. Many Roman Catholic priests and learned doctors of theology attempted to convert the Waldenses. Some admitted that the average Waldensian church member knew more Scripture than they did. One Roman Catholic priest, returning from a mission to the Waldenses, stated that he had learned more Scripture conversing with them than he had in his formal theological training. Theological professors from the University at Sorbonne acknowledged that the children of the Waldenses were better trained in the Scriptures than they were!

The Waldenses recognized other independent churches which preached the gospel as being from the Lord. They formally united with the surviving Arnoldists in southern Italy.

They produced several written confessions of faith that made their general beliefs very clear. Those confessions also attracted the attention of the Roman Catholic Church and were used as the basis for persecuting them.

The French Waldenses were particularly noted for opposing the idea of infant baptism and were repeatedly singled out by the established church for criticism over their refusal to baptize infants.

Persecution after persecution was directed at the Waldenses. Tens of thousands were slain over several centuries; however, there were always the Alps. The Alps touched Switzerland, Italy, France, and Germany. The Waldenses fled to the Alps so often that the mountains and the Waldenses became synonymous in the minds of many people. The Waldenses developed their own villages, complete with schools and hospitals in the mountains.

The Waldenses were careful to try to work out peaceful arrangements with the governments near them. They were very careful about paying their taxes — even paying them during times when they were being persecuted. They held numerous meetings with government and church officials to explain their positions. They often allowed Roman Catholic priests to come into areas they controlled and preach to them (in the name of religious liberty). There is not one record of a Roman Catholic priest having any substantial success on one of those missions. They finally had to cease those practices because the priests often served as advance scouts for persecuting military forces. The Waldenses published statements clearly explaining their positions.

For all their effort to get along with local government, they usually were not successful. When they were ordered to stop preaching, they refused. When their church buildings were destroyed, they assembled in mountains, valleys, and forests. When they were ordered to stop distributing the Scriptures, they continued anyway. The Waldenses translated the Scriptures into at least six different languages and spread copies throughout central Europe. Other Baptist groups such as the Albigenses and the Petrobrusians often used translations provided by the Waldenses. When the Waldenses were ordered to baptize their infants, they defied those orders from the surrounding church states.

The Waldenses attracted special persecution because of their separate schools. They believed that all education was religious and that they had the responsibility to train their own children. In many areas there were no schools or very weak schools. They were determined that their children should learn to read so they could study the Bible for themselves. Because of this, most Waldenses were literate during a time when few could read. They even taught their female children to read at a time when this was unheard of in society at large. Many people were jealous at the success of their educational programs and special attempts were made to destroy their schools. (Things haven't changed much!)

Their enemies often said that the most important verse to the Waldenses was, "We ought to obey God rather than man." Their doctrines of separation of church and state, sole authority of Scripture, and soul liberty forced them to defy government when it tried to interfere with their religious liberty.

At times, the Waldenses organized to defend themselves against their persecutors. They fought many pitched battles, and often won victories against seemingly overwhelming odds. However, the Roman Catholic state governments could always raise new armies to send against them. They finally realized that trying to cooperate with government would not work in their situation. It was also obvious that trying to militarily defeat the rampaging Roman Catholic armies was not possible. They returned to their policy of retreating to the Alps during times of persecution.

The Waldenses were also very missionary-minded, and

records prove their missionaries went to many lands. Waldensian missionaries were among the first settlers in Brazil, and they traveled to Scandinavia, Greece, Russia, and northern Africa.

Many Waldenses identified themselves with the Anabaptist movements of the Sixteenth Century. This is one reason that those movements grew so quickly. Others joined the Protestant reformers during the same period. The Waldenses of northern Italy remained a distinct movement and continue to this day. They are evangelical, but most have not continued to be Baptist. They are normally tolerated in northern Italy, but as recently as the 1970's, Waldenses have been arrested for preaching the gospel in Rome!

All evangelicals, especially independent Baptists, owe much to the courageous Waldenses.

Chapter 17

Rise of the Anabaptists

"Many are my persecutors and mine enemies; yet do I not decline from thy testimonies. I beheld the transgressors, and was grieved; because they kept not thy word" (Psalms 119:157-158).

John Hus was the pastor of a Roman Catholic Church in Prague (modern day Czechoslovakia, then a German state). He obtained copies of John Wycliffe's books, studied them, and soon adopted his views. This drove Hus to a serious study of the New Testament, resulting in his personal conversion. As Hus continued to study, he became convinced of a number of the Baptist distinctives. His fiery preaching attracted a great following. The Roman Church was at this time split between two competing Popes and little attention was given to persecuting people — like Hus — who strayed from Roman Catholic doctrine and dogma. Hus was free to preach the truth for several years.

Finally, the established church reconciled its difficulties, and shortly thereafter Hus was excommunicated. He then began to boldly preach separation of church and state and was forced into exile where he devoted himself to writing doctrinal books. He accepted a safe-conduct to the Roman Catholic Council of Constance where he determined to share his views on salvation, the sole authority of Scripture, and separation of church and state. However, since he was a "heretic," he did not deserve to be treated honestly, so he was condemned by the council and burned at the stake!

Any Roman Catholic could lie under oath, anytime, in

any place, if it helped the Roman Catholic Church! Hus was a "heretic" to the Roman Catholics because he rejected the mass, believed in preaching anywhere — not only in church buildings, denied the infallibility of the Pope, and said that Cardinals and Popes were unnecessary! So, the reasonable thing (reasonable to blood-thirsty religious tyrants) was to burn Hus at the stake.

Churches around Prague deserted Roman Catholicism in large groups and divided into two groups — Utraquists, who stood for the *final* authority of Scripture, and Taborites, who taught the *sole* authority of Scripture. They brought freedom to an entire region, pulling them from the established church. They formed an army together and successfully defeated invading Roman Catholic armies. The blind Taborite general, John Zizka, is still considered one of the most brilliant military leaders of all time. Again and again he defeated larger Roman Catholic armies. As long as the two groups worked together, they were never defeated. The amount of territory they controlled continued to increase.

Several doctrinal disputes arose between the Taborites, who were Baptist, and the Utraquists who were not. The Roman Catholic Church encouraged the Utraquists to return to the established church, promising them the right to practice and preach as they wished as long as they acknowledged the Pope as a spiritual authority. Incredibly, they agreed, and civil war broke out between the Utraquists and the Taborites. The Utraquists received military aid from Roman Catholic states, and the Taborites were defeated. The region around Prague was returned to Roman Catholic control.

The surviving Taborites united with the local Waldenses and formed a group called *Unitas Fratum*. Each church was independent and committed to the sole authority of Scripture and other Baptist principles. Over the decades, many Utraquists repented of their association with Roman Catholicism and joined the *Unitas Fratum*. From this group came both the Moravians and the German Anabaptists. In a letter explaining their position to Erasmus, the Taborites said, "They receive no other rule than the Bible and admit none into their communion till they be dipped in water."

In the Fifteenth Century, a bold Italian priest named Savonarola began to preach justification by faith, sole authority of Scripture, and against the corruption of the Roman Catholic Church. He had all Italy in an uproar, and to keep him quiet Pope Alexander VI offered him a bribe: a cardinal's hat! The brave preacher replied that he would take "a red hat," but one made out of blood. He said that another Pope, Boniface VIII, was a wicked man who began his reign like a fox and ended it like a dog! The Pope's emissaries tied him to a stake, burned him to death, and threw his ashes into the Arno River. His last words were, "Jesus, Jesus."

Savonarola was a brave preacher; however, there is one strange facet of his life: He was a devout Roman Catholic to the day he died! This is a good example of a great man who held on to a tradition that was enslaving millions of souls. No one knows whether he stayed in the Roman Church because of family, associates, or whatever. God says, ". . . Come out from among them, and be ye separate . . ." (II Corinthians 6:17).

It is interesting to speculate on where Savonarola's deep sense of loyalty to the sole authority of Scripture would have taken him had he been allowed to live and study the Scriptures for many years.

In Germany, a group called the "Brethren of Common Life" arose. They were committed to the sole authority of Scripture, and they founded schools to train people in the Scriptures. They hoped to reform Roman Catholicism from within. One of their most famous leaders, John of Wessel, taught justification by faith, the priesthood of all believers, and challenged the authority of the Roman Catholic Church. He was cast into prison and died there.

Another well-known member of the Brethren of Common Life was Erasmus. His work on the Greek New Testament and producing the *Textus Receptus* greatly influenced

Tyndale and the translation of the Scripture into English. Luther translated the New Testament into German from his text. It is the Greek text used in the translation of the King James Bible.

The Brethren of Common Life were not Baptists, and they did not come out of Roman Catholicism to start independent churches. However, many of the products of their schools carried their teachings further toward the Baptists than the leaders planned. Many of their graduates became Anabaptists. Erasmus was even accused of being an Anabaptist. He denied this, but he spoke against the persecution of the Anabaptists and acknowledged that he had many close friends among them.

By the Fifteenth and Sixteenth Centuries, the name *Anabaptist* came into common use to describe independent churches. The term *Anabaptist* had been a common theological term for centuries. It meant re-baptizer. It usually referred to those who rejected infant baptism and baptized believers upon their profession of faith. This was the normal practice of most independent churches. All Baptists were thus called Anabaptists, but not all Anabaptists were Baptists. (Some denied some of the other Baptist distinctives.) Unfortunately, in Germany, the name *Anabaptist* came to be applied to anyone who taught separation of church and state even if they didn't practice believers' baptism. This created a great amount of confusion.

It is important to understand that the Anabaptists were not a new movement. Some church historians claim that Anabaptists were only another group that developed during the Reformation, but Anabaptists did not see themselves that way at all. They claimed a direct line back to the Apostles, and there is abundant historical evidence to document their claim. This has caused many honest historians, though not Baptists, to acknowledge their antiquity.

The Lutheran historian, Mosheim, wrote:

> *In the first place the Mennonites are not altogether in the wrong, when they boast of a descent*

from these Waldenses, Petrobrusians, and others, who are usually styled witnesses for the truth before Luther. Prior to the age of Luther, there lay concealed in almost every country of Europe, but especially in Bohemia, Moravia, Switzerland, and Germany, very many persons in whose minds were deeply rooted that principle which the Waldenses, Wyclifites, and the Husites maintained, some more covertly and others more openly; namely, that the kingdom which Christ set up on the earth, or the visible church, is an assembly of holy persons; and ought therefore to be entirely free from not only ungodly persons and sinners, but from all institutions of human device against ungodliness. This principle lay at the foundation which was the source of all that was new and singular in the religion of the Mennonites; and the greatest part of their singular opinions, as is well attested, were approved some centuries before Luther's time, by those who had such views of the church of Christ.

The Quaker, Robert Barclay, wrote:

We shall afterwards show the rise of the Anabaptists took place prior to the Reformation of the Church of England, and there are also reasons for believing that on the continent of Europe small hidden Christian societies, who have held many of the opinions of the Anabaptists, have existed from the times of the Apostles. In the sense of the direct transmission of Divine Truth, and the true nature of spiritual religion, it seems probable that these churches have a lineage or succession more ancient than that of the Roman Church.

That is an incredible admission from a non-Baptist historian!

Several Roman Catholic councils condemned the Anabaptist movement as being hundreds of years old. A Roman Catholic cardinal, Cardinal Hosius, who participated in the famous Council of Trent in 1560 A.D. wrote:

If the truth of religion were to be judged by the readiness and boldness of which a man of any sect shows in suffering, then the opinion and persuasion of no sect can be truer and surer than that of the Anabaptists, since there have been none for these 1,200 years past, that have been more generally punished or that have more cheerfully and steadfastly undergone, and even offered themselves to, the most cruel sorts of punishment than these people.

Even Luther acknowledged that the Anabaptist movement was not new and that it had existed for hundreds of years in Germany. He acknowledged that John Hus should be considered an Anabaptist.

The great scientist, Sir Isaac Newton, was also a theological student and a church historian. His study led him to state that it was his conviction that "the Baptists were the only Christians who had not symbolized with Rome."

It is very fair and historically accurate to understand that Baptist history may be remembered in stages according to the names by which Baptist preachers were called.

- The first stage is the apostolic and New Testament Churches and their direct successors.
- This stage led to the Cathari, Celtic Christians, Montanists, Novatians, Donatists, and Paulicians.
- These groups led directly to the third stage: Waldenses, Lollards, Albigenses, Petrobrusians, Henricians, Arnoldists, Berengarians, Taborites, and Bogomils.
- In the fourth stage, preachers of Baptist convictions were called *Anabaptists*.
- Now they are called *Baptists*.

In 1819, two Dutch theologians, both members of the Reformed Church, made a study of the claims of Dutch Baptists to apostolic origin. That study led them to conclude:

> *We have now seen that the Baptists who were formerly called Anabaptists, and in later times Mennonites, were the original Waldenses, and who have long in the history of the church received the honor of that origin. On this account the Baptists may be considered as the only Christian community which has stood since the days of the apostles, and as a Christian society which has preserved pure the doctrines of the Gospel through all ages.*

So it is not only Baptists who teach a long line back to the New Testament; even those unfriendly to Baptists admit that fact.

Chapter 18

Baptist Ideas Help Create the Reformation

"Take, my brethren, the prophets, who have spoken in the name of the Lord, for an example of suffering affliction, and of patience" (James 5:10).

The Sixteenth Century saw Roman Catholic power shaken so strongly that it has never recovered. Roman Catholicism permanently lost control of Scandinavia, England, Switzerland, and Holland and was forced to share control in Germany. Its authority was seriously challenged everywhere on the European continent. Even where it maintained some semblance of control, its power would never be unlimited again. This period is usually referred to as the Reformation, and there were many factors which helped to create it.

The failure of the Roman Catholic Church to maintain one organization caused questions in the mind of many people. There were constantly rival Popes, anti-Popes, and splits within church leadership. When more than one church leader was claiming to be the one true Pope it created much confusion. During the period called the "Great Schism," there were actually four rival Popes, each appointed by a different church council. Many quiet jokes were told at the expense of common respect for the papacy. The total failure of the Crusades also caused people to question the infallibility of the church and the Pope. If the Pope really represented the will of God, why had the expeditions to Palestine failed so miserably? Either God was powerless or the Roman Catholic Church did not really speak for Him.

The inability of the established church to destroy the independent churches also raised great questions in the minds of many. All the force of governments, armies, papal police, and paid assassins could not extinguish the evangelical and Baptist groups. Hundreds of thousands of hangings, burnings, stabbings, and beheadings could not stop the independents. Burned cities, towns, and villages only drove them to the mountains, but such measures could not destroy them.

Reasonable people also began to question why the Roman Catholic Church had such hatred for people who studied the Bible or were independent thinkers. There are many testimonies to the fact that Baptists (and other non-conformists) usually led the purest lives and were the least offensive in their conduct. Why did the established church hate them so much? Reasonable people began to question the morality of the organized church just as they began to question its power. The testimony of the Baptist martyrs haunted the Roman Catholic Church during the Sixteenth Century.

Certainly the revival of learning in Europe during the Fifteenth and Sixteenth Centuries challenged the church. This *Renaissance* caused people to learn to read, to study, and to think for themselves. This was called *humanism*, but it was very different from the secular humanism of the Twentieth Century. The humanists of the Renaissance were simply setting themselves free from the official traditions of the Roman Catholic Church. This led many of them to study the Scripture directly.

Erasmus was a humanist (as was John Calvin), who studied the Scripture directly. Many of the Swiss Anabaptist leaders were humanists. This led them to study the Scripture directly, which led them to the Waldenses, Petrobrusians, and Albigenses of the Alps. (Those who call themselves humanists today are implying that they are free from any influence of God and the Bible.) As people began to ask "Why?" they realized that the Roman Catholic

Church was obviously short on answers. When people began to ask, "Where is that in the Bible?" the Roman Catholic Church often had no answer.

When people during the Renaissance began to study the Bible for themselves, they usually studied the Latin Vulgate translation. As the literacy rate rose, people wanted to read the Bible in their own language. By the time of Luther, the male literacy rate in Germany had risen from ten percent to over 50 percent! The Waldenses had translated the Scriptures into most of the languages of Europe, and copies of their translations became highly desired. Two hundred years after Luther's translation of the Bible, the Waldenses' German translation was still widely used in Germany. If it had not been for the Baptist Waldenses, most Europeans would not have had any chance to study the Scriptures in their own language.

There were many influences which contributed to the revival of learning in Europe. Kings and rulers wanted to build national unity by getting people to read and think in their own language. Many humanists wanted to encourage the study of the Greek classics. The Roman Catholic Church was no longer powerful enough to inhibit learning, and one of the most powerful influences was the desire to read the Scriptures. The independent churches had influenced so many people that this created a tremendous desire to read the Bible. The doctrine of sole authority of Scripture is of limited value to an illiterate population. Without a doubt, the Baptist doctrine of sole authority of Scripture did much to pave the way for the Renaissance (revival of learning) and the Reformation period in Europe.

The widespread dissatisfaction with the Roman Catholic clergy was also heavily influenced by the existence of the independent churches. The priests and monks who dealt with the common people were often illiterate and had no Bible or theological training. Their primary roles were social and political — not religious. It was very common for them not to even make any pretense of piety, spiritual concern, or even basic morality. It was this fact that first opened the eyes of Martin Luther that something was wrong with the established church. This was the main point of Zwingli's call to revolt in Switzerland, and it was the major theme of the Reformers in England.

Certainly, independent churches also had scandals among their preachers during this period; however, because they were independent, they could deal with their problems. They did not have to accept a preacher just because he had been ordained by an authority to which the local church had to answer. Independent churches could simply remove a pastor who did not live up to their standards. Their pastors also had Bibles to study and usually had some form of theological training — often one-on-one training from another pastor. They were usually the most educated person in their congregation. The Roman Catholic priests suffered by comparison.

The Baptist doctrine of the independence of the local church was a doctrine that contributed greatly to the complaints of the common people against the corruption within the established church.

Without a doubt, the invention of printing was a major factor in the arrival and spread of the Reformation. This became a reality in 1450 when Johann Gutenberg perfected printing with movable type. In 1455, he produced the Gutenberg Bible, known by some as the 42-line Bible because it had 42 lines per page.

Printing dramatically increased the opportunities of teachers of any persuasion to spread their message, and Baptists were very quick to use the printed page. Tracts, pamphlets, and books poured out to the general population from Baptist sources. When persecution limited the independent churches from publishing, the Lutheran and Reformed Churches took the lead in religious publishing. Later, in the Sixteenth Century, the Roman Catholic Church made a major effort at providing printed material for the masses.

The Baptist doctrines of soul liberty and the priesthood of each believer influenced the Baptist attitude toward publishing. While other religious movements tried to advance by appealing to religious or political leaders, Baptists appealed to everyone. Some historians believe that if the Protestants (and later the Roman Catholics) had not turned to publishing, the Baptists would have become the dominant group in Europe.

In modern America, where everyone is used to having their own opinions about religion, it is difficult to imagine the influence that these doctrines had. People who had always been told not to think or read or question were now being told that they stood equal before God. People who were used to being told that they were too insignificant to have their own opinions were now being appealed to as individuals who could think for themselves. It is no wonder that the common people flocked to the Baptists and other independent assemblies. This forced the Protestant, and even the Roman Catholic, leadership to directly appeal to the common people.

Baptist ideas had such influence on the general population of Europe during the late Fifteenth and early Sixteenth Centuries that they were a major force in creating the Reformation. Even Luther and Zwingli worked with Baptists during the early days of the Reformation; however, Baptist ideas did not immediately win the day. The bloody suppression of Baptists and other independents by both the Protestant reformers and Roman Catholic leadership brought all of Europe (except Holland) under the control of state churches. However, in a very real sense, the Baptists did win. Today, the idea of individual liberty, personal religion, and separation of church and state (or at least religious toleration) are common in Europe. Even in Roman Catholic countries like Spain and Italy, it is relatively easy to defy the established church. Many Protestants even claim to be the ones who brought personal liberty and separation of church and state to Europe. This claim, of course, completely ignores the historical record. Protestant leadership fought those Baptist ideas, but they were eventually forced to capitulate.

The heritage of the Baptists and other independents was a major force in creating the concept of freedom that the western world enjoys today. Every non-Baptist should tip his hat every time he passes a Baptist church because he owes his freedom to the Baptists.

Chapter 19

The Faithful Baptist Witness

"Who through faith subdued kingdoms, wrought righteousness, obtained promises, stopped the mouths of lions, Quenched the violence of fire, escaped the edge of the sword, out of weakness were made strong, waxed valiant in fight, turned to flight the armies of the aliens. Women received their dead raised to life again: and others were tortured, not accepting deliverance; that they might obtain a better resurrection: And others had trial of cruel mockings and scourgings, yea, moreover of bonds and imprisonment: They were stoned, they were sawn asunder, were tempted, were slain with the sword: they wandered about in sheepskins and goatskins; being destitute, afflicted, tormented; (Of whom the world was not worthy:) they wandered in deserts, and in mountains, and in dens and caves of the earth. And these all, having obtained a good report through faith, received not the promise: God having provided some better thing for us, that they without us should not be made perfect" (Hebrews 11:33-40).

We have not yet studied a single Baptist group which did not endure violent and brutal persecution. The most famous of the persecutors of the Baptists that we have studied include:

- Nero,
- Marcus Aurelius,
- Justinian,
- Empress Theodora,

- Diocletian,
- Pope Innocent III,
- Charlemagne, and
- Augustine.

Persecutors of Baptists which we have not yet studied include:

- Martin Luther,
- John Calvin,
- Ulrich Zwingli,
- Henry VIII,
- Bloody Mary,
- Queen Elizabeth,
- Louis XIV,
- Charles I,
- Charles II,
- Napoleon,
- Adolf Hitler,
- Joseph Stalin,
- Mao Tse Tung, and
- Fidel Castro.

The list of persecutors of Baptists reads like a *Who's Who* in world history. Baptists have been persecuted by:

- pagan tribes,
- the Roman Empire,
- the Roman Catholic Church,
- militant Moslems,
- Protestants, and
- Communists.

Baptists have been persecuted by

- the Jewish faith,
- the Roman Catholic established church,
- the Moslems,
- Lutherans,
- Reformed Churches,
- the Church of England,
- the Church of Scotland,
- the Puritans of Massachusetts Bay Colony, and

- the Anglican Church of the colonies of Virginia, North and South Carolina, and others.

Baptists have been persecuted by:
- emperors,
- kings,
- the Sanhedrin,
- priests,
- Popes,
- preachers,
- military leaders,
- dictators,
- queens,
- sheiks, and
- ayatollahs (supposed Moslem holy teachers).

There have been wide scale persecutions of large Baptist groups in:
- Asia,
- northern Africa,
- virtually every country of Europe,
- Central and South America, and
- many of the early American colonies.

Baptists have been:
- crucified,
- beheaded,
- burned at the stake,
- thrown to wild animals,
- starved,
- stabbed,
- stoned,
- beaten,
- drowned, and
- tortured to death.

There seem to have been several waves of persecution directed against Baptists (and often others).
- The first wave was primarily Jewish.

The Sanhedrin, meeting in Jerusalem, put Christians to death in Israel and harassed them throughout the Roman

Empire.

- A second wave involved local persecutions throughout the Roman Empire and perhaps other regions as well.

The teachings of Christianity threatened the interests of false religions and petty dictators.

- A third wave began as Christianity attracted the attention of the Roman Empire.

Various Caesars tried to destroy that which they could not understand or control. The first three waves were, of course, directed at Christians in general.

The next wave of persecution had an entirely different character to it. This wave came repeatedly throughout the Dark Ages.

- The Roman Catholic Church persecuted Baptists and other independents in the name of Christ.

They claimed that this was necessary to preserve "the one true church."

- A fifth wave of persecution came during the Reformation as Catholics, Protestants, and Anglicans united to destroy anyone who spoke for the idea of religious liberty.

Even though these groups were bitter enemies, they often cooperated in their attempts to destroy anyone who advocated separation of church and state.

- A sixth wave has come because of Communist advances in the Twentieth Century.

Again, this form of persecution has been directed against all forms of true Christianity. Christians have been killed by the millions by Communists in:

- Russia,
- eastern Europe,
- mainland China,
- Ethiopia,
- Cuba,
- southeast Asia, and
- Nicaragua.

This has been by far the bloodiest, most brutal, and largest persecution of Christians in history.

Famous Baptist martyrs have included:

- John the Baptist,
- Stephen,
- most of the Apostles,
- early church fathers like Polycarp and Irenaeus,
- Peter of Bruys,
- Constantine of the Paulicians,
- Arnold of Bresica,
- Felix Manz,
- Balthasar Hubmaier, and
- George Blaurock.

Men like Peter Waldo and Menno Simons died in exile.

The imprisonment of men like John Bunyan, Melchoir Hoffman, and Henry of Lausanne stand out in the story of the struggle for religious freedom.

No one can say how many have died for their Baptist convictions over the last two thousand years, but it is safe to say that the number figures into the millions!

It is not easy to understand why the Baptists have been hated so. J. M. Cramp, in his *Baptist History*, explains:

> *The Baptists of the Sixteenth Century, generally, were a goodly, upright, honourable race. They hated no man. But all men hated them. And why? Because they testified against the abominations of the times, and wished to accomplish changes which would indeed have revolutionized society, because it was constructed on anti-Christian principles, but which were in accordance with the Word of God. An outcry was raised against them, as if they were "the off-scouring of all things," and their blood was poured out like water. Even the Reformers wrote and acted against them. The writers of that age searched out the most degrading and insulting epithets that the language afforded, and applied*

them with malignant gratification. Latimer speaks of the "pernicious" and "devilish" opinions of the Baptists. Hooper calls those opinions "damnable." Bacon inveighs against the "wicked," "apish Anabaptists," "foxish hypocrites," that "damnable sect," "liars," "bloody murderers both of soul and body," whose religious system he denounces as a "pestiferous plague," with many other foul-mouthed expressions which we will not copy. Bullinger designates them as "obstinate," "rebellious," "brain-sick," "frantic," "filthy knaves." Zwingli speaks of the "pestiferous seed of their doctrine," their "hypocritical humility," their speech, "more bitter than gall." But enough of this. These men could, notwithstanding all, appeal to those who witnessed their sufferings, and boldly declare, with the ax or the stake in view, none venturing to contradict, that they were not put to death for any evil deeds, but solely for the sake of the Gospel.

The simple Biblical faith of Baptists has testified to the errors within other religious systems. Their cries for freedom — personal and religious — have angered those who ruled over other men.

The study of Baptist history makes one vital truth clear: There will often be a terrible price to pay to stand for the truth. There are no promises that it will be easy to be faithful. It is often difficult for Americans to grasp this truth because for two hundred years we have had the privilege of obeying our own religious convictions, running our own lives, making our own decisions and planning our own futures. There has, at times, been harassment from civil government, but normally there is not. There are no guarantees that this will always be reality.

This period of freedom is virtually an historic curiosity. It runs counter to all the normal lessons of history. Human beings normally will use any method available to keep their faults from being exposed. In 1521, William Reublin, an Anabaptist preacher in Switzerland, began to openly preach Bible truth. By name, he called on the Pope, bishops, and local Catholic clergy to disprove his doctrinal positions from the Bible. Rather than answer his challenge, they banished him from the area, but he moved to another Swiss town and repeated the same procedure. He was banished again. This took place a third time, and he was finally executed. When laws, harassment, and banishment would not silence him, they thought execution was only reasonable. After all, according to tyrants, "heretics" do not have a right to live. Reublin had been banished twice by Catholics, once by Protestants, and was finally executed by Protestants.

Often, persecutors have expressed great sorrow at being "forced" to persecute non-conformists, and having "no other option." Jerome Bolsec, a physician in Geneva, Switzerland, began to challenge John Calvin's explanation of predestination and election. (It is debatable whether or not Bolsec was an Anabaptist.) When Calvin could not convince him to change his doctrine, he and the city council of Geneva had Bolsec arrested. After a long trial, he was banished from Geneva for life. Not long after Bolsec was banished, Michael Servetus was executed in Geneva for holding "heretical" views on the deity of Christ (he, in fact, denied the deity of Christ.) and baptism (he was opposed to infant baptism). Calvin expressed great sorrow at both incidents. He could not (or would not) allow people to disagree with his thinking, so he had no choice but to participate in these and other persecutions. There is something about a person's pride that makes it difficult to tolerate dissent. That is why no one person can be trusted with unlimited power — not even evangelical preachers like Martin Luther, John Calvin, or Ulrich Zwingli.

Calvin and Luther both put their stamp of approval upon the execution of Baptists, and Zwingli actually participated in such persecution. Whether it is a Roman Emperor, local chief, fascist dictator, royal monarch, Catholic Pope or bishop, or Protestant reformer, no human can be trusted with control of the personal lives, religious beliefs, or conscience of other human beings. Baptists stand out in the annals of religious and secular history as being free from ever persecuting others. This is not because they are immune to the temptations of pride and human nature, but because their system of separation of church and state allows everyone religious freedom. God gave us this approach to government and faith because He knew the weaknesses of men.

The truth can never be suppressed by laws, decrees, arrests, harassments, or banishment, and those who wish to suppress freedom of speech, religion, and personal liberty must always be willing to resort to execution — and they have, down through the ages.

Throughout history there has always been a handful of brave political leaders who stood for personal freedom. Some men stand out as having struggled for religious and personal liberty:

- William the Silent,
- Henry of Navarre,
- William III of Orange,
- Oliver Cromwell, and
- Patrick Henry
- [among many, many others.]

Their efforts helped to bring the blessings of personal and religious liberties to different groups for various periods of time. However, this is not the norm.

Baptists have been the ultimate challenge to tyranny in every form. The only effective way to silence Baptists has been to kill them; thus, Baptist history has indeed been written in a "Trail of Blood." The story of brave men and women teaching the sole authority of Scripture, believer's baptism, independent churches, separation of church and state, priesthood of all believers, and soul liberty is a story of bloodshed.

- The blood of the Celtic Christians was shed all over the British Isles;
- The mideast is stained with the blood of the early Christians, the Paulicians, and missionaries from the First Century until our modern era.
- Europe has seen the bloody deaths of Montanists, Novatians, Albigenses, Cathari, Bogomils, Waldenses, Arnoldists, Petrobrusians, Henricians, Anabaptists, and Baptists.
- The history of the English tradition of freedom is marred by deaths of Lollards, Anabaptists, and Baptists.

Even in our modern era, Baptists are not safe in much of the world, for example, in Communist countries like China, North Korea, and Cuba, and most Moslem countries. There are serious rumblings of government discontent with independent Baptists and other non-conformists in our "western world" — especially the United States. No one can tell how long modern Baptists in America will enjoy our unparalleled period of freedom to believe, teach, and practice Bible truth.

The past history of Baptists has been written in blood, so it is wise to face honestly whatever the future may hold. We should pray for continued freedom and blessings. We should work diligently to maintain the freedoms that we now possess, but we should also be spiritually prepared for whatever circumstances we may have to face. Baptist history has indeed been a "Trail of Blood." Our future may likewise be a "Trail of Blood."

Chapter 20

The Reformation

"These things have I spoken unto you, that ye should not be offended. They shall put you out of the synagogues: yea, the time cometh, that whosoever killeth you will think that he doeth God service. And these things will they do unto you, because they have not known the Father, nor me" (John 16:1-3).

The religious scene in Europe was in turmoil at the beginning of the Sixteenth Century, and this fact set the stage for an historic upheaval that resulted in major political and religious changes. The most important historical figure of this century was certainly Martin Luther.

In 1505, Luther was admitted to a monastery, beginning a deep study of the Christian life and the doctrine of the established church. He was looking for something to bring peace to his troubled soul. For 20 years he had sought unsuccessfully for peace through good works, penance, the Roman Catholic Church, and academic study. Finally, he became a teacher in Biblical Studies at Wittenberg University without finding personal satisfaction.

In the course of his studies, Luther came to an understanding of justification by faith, and he began to teach it to others, finding a number of people who were enthusiastic about that truth. Luther gave testimony that he had been converted to Christ and had personally experienced justification by faith in the finished work of Christ.

The Roman Catholic teaching about indulgences was a long-established tradition that went contrary to the Bible teaching of faith. Indulgences meant that money could be used to purchase release from time in purgatory for an individual or his loved ones, and it was a major part of the Roman Catholic religion. It was also a major part of the Roman Catholic financial program. Luther was teaching justification by faith at Wittenberg at just the time the most widespread Roman Catholic indulgence program came to Germany.

A Roman Catholic priest, Johann Tetzel, was now claiming to offer the ultimate indulgence: If you paid the right sum of money, your dead relatives could immediately be released from purgatory and admitted to Heaven. This was such an outrageous claim that many people openly opposed Tetzel. Luther wrote his famous "Ninety-five Theses" (points to consider) and nailed them to the church door at Wittenberg. Those points covered justification by faith, the authority of Scripture, and attacked both the concept of indulgences in general and the recent fund-raising drive by Tetzel in particular. His Ninety-five Theses were copied, printed, and spread throughout Germany. This served as a catalyst to the already widespread frustrations with the Roman Catholic Church. Defiance of the church became common, public, and normal throughout Germany.

For several years, Luther engaged in theological debate with Roman Catholic leadership until his arrest was ordered on the basis of "heresy." A German nobleman hid and protected him for several months while he translated the New Testament into German and worked out his formal doctrinal positions. Throughout Germany, nobles and common people broke with the Roman Catholic Church. Some opposed Roman Catholicism for religious reasons, some political, and some economic. Independent churches flourished and, at first, joined the followers of Luther in a struggle for religious liberty.

Two things changed this direction. First, the Peasants' Revolt upset many German nobles. Led by Thomas Munzer, many German peasants rebelled, trying to establish a free country. They were logically applying the principles of personal and religious freedom that both Luther and the independent preachers were teaching. The peasants expected Luther to join them (or even lead them), and most were shocked when he stood with the tyrannical nobility! The Peasants' Revolt was quickly crushed. Because so many independent church people were involved in the revolt, the nobility — both Roman Catholic and Lutheran — became especially fearful of religious liberty.

Secondly, because the churches had been the source of most social organization, all areas of life were in upheaval. Even the most anti-Catholic people began to look for some way to reorganize society. Luther abandoned the concept of religious freedom, and began to organize Lutheranism as an alternate state church to Roman Catholicism. This was very satisfactory to most nobles because it prevented religious liberty (which they feared would lead to political liberty), and it gave them a wedge against the power of the Roman Catholic Church.

Many nobles simply offered allegiances to whichever state church would cooperate with them the most. Many regions changed loyalties often as new deals were struck between princes and church leaders. Each Prince expected the citizens of his state to support the religion that he supported. Independent churches and preachers were systematically destroyed by both groups.

The story of the next hundred years of German history is the struggle, both military and political, of the Lutheran and Roman Catholic state churches for control of the various regions of Germany. Charles V, Emperor of Germany, seemed powerless to hold his nation together. Fear of an invasion of Germany by the Moslems (who already controlled parts of eastern Europe) finally led to a truce between Roman Catholics and Lutherans. Finally, a peace was achieved which allowed the citizens of Germany to be either Roman Catholic or Lutheran, but nothing else. Even today, citizens of Germany are required to tithe to either the Lutheran or Roman Catholic Church.

The open rebellion against Roman Catholicism quickly spread to other countries until no European country was untouched by it. In Switzerland, independents and reformers fought for freedom from Roman Catholicism. In fact, there were 21 military campaigns in a seven-year period. Most of Switzerland became Protestant, led by Ulrich Zwingli in the formation of an evangelical Protestant state church. Zwingli had trouble with his former allies — the independents. Soon the Protestant church was persecuting the independents even more severely than the Catholics had. Zwingli was killed in the last battle against Roman Catholic forces, and Switzerland became Protestant.

In Flanders (modern Holland, Belgium, and Luxembourg), civil war broke out between Roman Catholics, Protestants, and independents. The non-Catholics won control of modern Holland, and the rest of the area remained under Roman control. Under the leadership of William the Silent, a state church was not established in Holland, and religious liberty became the law there. Evangelicals, independents, and Protestants began to grow in influence in both Spain and Italy; however, they never became a major military or political force in either country. Toward the end of the Sixteenth Century, those movements were crushed by persecution.

A Frenchman, John Calvin, became a very important Bible teacher and leader in Switzerland. He popularized a theological system with a strong emphasis on predestination, infant baptism, and a church-dominated state. This system is usually remembered by his name, Calvinism. His abilities as a thinker, teacher, writer, and leader are without question; however, his system was very different from the Baptists. While both groups agreed on the fundamentals of the Christian faith, they disagreed on every point of the Baptist distinctives (except the Lord's Supper and, perhaps, the priesthood of all believers). Calvin's system soon became the dominant belief among the Swiss Protestants.

Calvin's ideas spread to France, and his followers soon became the most visible group of Protestants in France.

Several members of the nobility, including one queen and two princesses, became Protestants. The Bourbon family, consisting of powerful nobles, became Protestants, and even the Roman Catholic Cardinal for France became a Protestant! His brother, Admiral Gaspard de Coligny, became a Protestant. De Coligny was considered the greatest military leader in France, and was very popular with both sailors and soldiers. His identification with the Protestants made Roman Catholic leadership careful about persecution. French Calvinists were called Huguenots.

It appeared as if the Protestants might take France as completely as they had Switzerland. Persecutions, executions, and assassinations were directed at the Protestants, and thousands of Waldenses, still active in southern France, were slain. Civil war broke out, and the Protestants were defeated — but not completely. They were given certain safe regions, and Coligny was given a position in the government. As the Protestants rose again in power, a new persecution took place, and on August 24, 1572, Coligny was assassinated. Following his death, an organized attack on Protestants took place throughout France with 50,000 killed in one day! This is remembered as the St. Bartholomew's Day Massacre. Civil war followed for almost 20 years.

Finally, peace came. Henry of Navarre, a Bourbon noble and military leader of the Protestants, made a deal with the Pope and the nobles. He converted to Catholicism and was recognized as king by everyone. He immediately granted religious freedom to all, and for 65 years France had religious liberty. Catholicism eventually became the established church again.

In Scotland, evangelical preachers like Patrick Hamilton and George Wishart stirred up the people against Roman Catholicism, and both were burned at the stake. Finally, the power of the Roman Catholic Church was broken by a coalition of Lutherans, Calvinists, and independents led by the Calvinist, John Knox. Soon Calvinism became the dominant religious movement, and a Calvinist state church was established in Scotland. However, independents were vigorously persecuted.

The Scandinavian countries (Denmark, Sweden, Norway, and Finland) were won over by the Lutherans and developed Lutheran state churches. Lutherans also temporarily gained control of Poland, which later returned to Roman Catholicism. Hungary turned briefly to religious freedom, then to Protestantism, and then was reclaimed by the Roman Catholic Church.

The Reformation of England was to play a major role in the founding of the United States. The Lollards and the English Bible translated by Tyndale had greatly prepared England for a break with Rome. Separatists, Baptists, and evangelicals within the established church opposed the supremacy of the Pope and Roman Catholic doctrine; however, the Reformation in England took on a decidedly political character.

Henry VIII wanted to divorce his first wife, Catherine (whose nephew, Charles V, was the leading supporter of the Pope in Europe and who was, herself, a devout Catholic). Henry wanted to marry Anne Boleyn who was from an evangelical family. Henry applied to the Pope for permission and, for six years, the Pope refused to give Henry a decision either way. Henry had been no friend of the Reformation, having been trained as a Catholic theologian. He had also written a book against Luther, and the Pope had awarded Henry the title, "Defender of the Faith." But now Henry rebelled against the Pope, declared himself to be the head of the Church of England, divorced Catherine, and married Anne. Protestants and Catholics competed for influence in the newly organized Church of England.

Henry's passions, his political dealings, and his theological leanings were in a constant state of change. He soon had Anne executed and eventually married four more wives: two Protestants, one Catholic, and one Lutheran. His leanings changed with each marriage. First one group and then another would dominate in the church. Within each change there was a wave of imprisonments, banishings, and executions. Henry had old friends, former trusted associates, and another wife put to death! William Tyndale was at first protected and then persecuted. He was later arrested in Antwerp (modern Belgium) and executed with the open approval of the English king. The course of the Church of England was not to be settled during Henry's lifetime.

His son, Edward VI, granted religious toleration and openly identified with the evangelicals within the church. He stopped the persecution of the Baptists which Henry had continued through all of his phases. Edward died just six years into his reign, and his sister, Mary, succeeded him. She tried to re-establish Roman Catholicism in England and is remembered as "Bloody Mary" because of her frequent execution of evangelical and Baptist preachers. She even had John Wycliffe's body dug up and his remains burned at the stake. She died five years into her reign and was followed to the throne by her sister, Elizabeth. Elizabeth put the Protestants back in control of the Church of England while evangelicals and Anglicans (who still taught much Catholic doctrine) had to share control of the church. She vigorously persecuted Baptists and other independents such as the Quakers.

The Quakers were a group started by George Fox whose parents were Baptists. He disagreed with the Baptists on sole authority of Scripture and baptism by immersion and is best remembered for his eloquent defense of separation of church and state.

The desire to escape persecution led many English to move to Holland or to colonize the territory west of the Atlantic Ocean (America). This drive for religious freedom was one of the most important factors in creating the United States of America.

Chapter 21

Swiss Anabaptists

"Beloved, think it not strange concerning the fiery trial which is to try you, as though some strange thing happened unto you: But rejoice, inasmuch as ye are partakers of Christ's sufferings; that, when his glory shall be revealed, ye may be glad also with exceeding joy" (1 Peter 4:12-13).

For many years before Zwingli and the Reformation became prominent in Switzerland, Baptist ideas had spread throughout the region. These ideas challenged a group of young men who regularly met in Zurich to study the Greek New Testament, comparing the Greek Scriptures with the concept of baptism of believers only. Most of the group came to the conclusion that this idea was the only one compatible with Scripture. Ulrich Zwingli, who was a member of the group, disagreed and no longer met with the study group on a regular basis.

This group of young students began to openly teach believers' baptism and also separation of church and state. Zwingli and the city council in Zurich ordered them to conform to the laws of baptism (infant baptism) and forbade them to hold group meetings. That evening, several members of the study group met in the home of Felix Manz. They pledged to be true to the New Testament and to teach its principles as widely as possible. Then, Conrad Grebel baptized George Blaurock who then baptized all of the other men present.

These men were not the first to teach believers' baptism in Switzerland. In fact, they all acknowledged that this truth had been taught for centuries by independent preachers and even, occasionally, by village priests. But these men were the first to gain the attention of all of Switzerland. The city council in Zurich began to openly persecute the Bible study group, but they continued to meet in secret and soon baptized many other believers.

Their critics began to call them *Anabaptists. Ana* means "again" in Greek. They were mocked for not accepting infant baptism and baptizing people again after their profession of faith in Christ. They often responded that they were not *Ana*baptists since what was being called infant "baptism" was not true baptism. Instead, they considered themselves Baptist people, practicing true baptism. Their usual term for each other was "Swiss Brethren."

Conrad Grebel and Felix Manz began to go from house to house sharing the gospel and encouraging people to trust Christ and accept believers' baptism. Hundreds were baptized including a well-known former Roman Catholic priest, Wolfgang Ulimann. The Zurich authorities began to arrest all the leaders of this movement, including Grebel and Manz. They were all sentenced to life imprisonment, and a new law was passed providing the death penalty for anyone baptizing by immersion. The proscribed punishment was to be death by drowning. One Reformed leader was quoted as saying, "They wish to be immersed so much, let us immerse them."

In the spring of 1526, Grebel and Manz, along with 12 other Anabaptists escaped from prison and quickly spread their teachings throughout Switzerland, Austria, and southern Germany. While living on the run and constantly in hiding, Grebel developed several illnesses and died in his weakened condition.

Manz and Blaurock were recaptured, but Blaurock escaped again. However, Manz was executed by drowning. He was tied to a long pole, submerged in a river, and then brought back above the surface. He was then asked if he would recant to save his life, but he answered, "No, I will be true to my belief." The authorities forced his mother to watch, and she cried, "Felix, do not recant. Do not recant!" This scene was repeated several times, and finally Manz was drowned.

Blaurock continued to preach throughout Switzerland and south Germany, and when an Anabaptist pastor, Michael Kurschner, was burned at the stake, Blaurock openly took his place in the church. He and a visiting evangelist were arrested, tortured, and burned at the stake.

Balthasar Hubmaier, a Roman Catholic Doctor of Theology, was personally converted and embarked on a study of the New Testament. He gradually became convinced that Baptist principles were Bible principles. He was arrested, tortured, and, at first, recanted his beliefs; however, he returned to teaching Baptist principles and was banished from Switzerland. He became a very influential Baptist preacher in Germany where he was martyred for his faith.

Michael Sattler, a converted Roman Catholic priest, wrote and spoke against public persecution for religious principles, and, when his secret meetings with Anabaptists were discovered, he was banished from Zurich. He openly identified with the Anabaptists, and began to preach throughout Switzerland and Germany. He was arrested, tried, and burned to death. Shortly thereafter, his wife was drowned by the authorities.

Anabaptists grew into a very large movement around the Swiss town of Berne. There they joined with the local descendants of the Waldenses. The local city council actively persecuted the Bernese Baptists, but the movement continued to grow. Persecution drove many of them to other countries, including Holland, and several of them were among the first Dutch colonists in the New World. There are still many Baptist churches around Berne today.

The Swiss Anabaptists were very clear in declaring that they were neither Catholic nor Protestant. Most of them were former Catholics who were being persecuted by Protestants (the Reformers). It was very easy for them to keep the distinction clear.

The Swiss Anabaptists were known for their emphasis in certain areas. The most significant, of course, was their teaching about baptism for believers only. They also strongly taught religious liberty and separation of church and state. While these teachings set them in constant opposition to the state church, several other teachings brought them great respect from the population in general.

These Anabaptists strongly emphasized the new commandment of love in John 13:34-35. They practiced that truth so much that when the general population thought of them they thought of love and commitment to one another. During the terrible persecutions, they often shared food, housing, money, and clothing with each other. This was so common that some outsiders thought that the Anabaptists did not believe in private property. Their writings show that they did believe in private property; however, their love made sharing a common daily experience. This testimony opened the doors of public respect to them even when they were being persecuted by the government.

The Anabaptists also taught godly living as a necessity for maintaining membership in the local church. Both the Roman Catholics and the Reformers taught that all citizens should be members of their church, but the Anabaptists expelled people from their churches for unrepentant immorality, false doctrine, and not being willing to resolve personal conflicts. This gave the Anabaptist churches a reputation for purity that the other churches did not have.

The Anabaptists agreed with both the Roman Catholics and the Protestants as to the absolute inspiration of Scripture, but they disagreed with the Roman Catholic teaching that the Church was the sole interpreter of Scripture. They disagreed with the Protestant idea that the Bible was to be interpreted by a group of scholarly teachers. They taught that every believer was indwelt by the Holy Spirit and could interpret the Bible for himself.

Anabaptists were also controversial for refusing to take

the prescribed oaths of loyalty to the state. Since the state was inseparable from the Reformed Church, the Anabaptists felt that the oath of loyalty interfered with their religious liberty. Most Anabaptists also refused to serve in the military because they felt that the church-controlled state was their enemy. Others refused to serve because they were pacifists.

Anabaptists also refused to have their marriage ceremonies performed by the officials of the state church, and this caused many people to believe that they were not married and were guilty of immorality. They felt that their lifetime pledge to each other, witnessed by a preacher and local witnesses, constituted Biblical marriage. The children of Anabaptists often had to grow up being considered illegitimate by those around them.

The Swiss Anabaptists made such an impact on the Swiss people that their ideas eventually began to take hold. Today, the Swiss have religious freedom and separation of church and state. The integrity, sacrifice, and faithfulness of the early Swiss Anabaptists led to the conversion of thousands in Switzerland, Holland, southern Germany, and Austria. Their descendants traveled to Russia with the gospel, and they helped pioneer the early settlements on the American frontier. They helped to settle once and for all the name to be attached to this movement — Baptist. Their answer of "Baptist, not Anabaptist," gave the Baptist movement the name it carries to this day.

Chapter 22

German Anabaptists

"If ye be reproached for the name of Christ, happy are ye; for the spirit of glory and of God resteth upon you: on their part he is evil spoken of, but on your part he is glorified. But let none of you suffer as a murderer, or as a thief, or as an evildoer, or as a busybody in other men's matters. Yet if any man suffer as a Christian, let him not be ashamed; but let him glorify God on this behalf" (1 Peter 4:14-16).

In 1524, in Augsburg, Germany, Hans Koch and Leonard Meyster were put to death for holding Baptist views. The purpose of their murders was to stop the Anabaptist influence in Augsburg, but this procedure failed miserably. By 1525, an Anabaptist church was organized in Augsburg and grew to 1,100 members by 1527. There were four pastors associated with this church:

- Hans Denck (the senior pastor or bishop),
- Balthasar Hubmaier (who had fled from Switzerland),
- Ludwig Hatzer, and
- Hans Hut.

Hubmaier had baptized Denck and had been instrumental in the formation of the church. It is clear, both from the writings of the church leaders and from the critics of the church, that the Augsburg church taught all of the Baptist distinctives. The church at Augsburg became a center for church planting and training preachers throughout southern Germany.

The church at Augsburg helped to start a church in

Strasbourg in 1526, and Hans Denck moved there by 1527 and assumed that pastorate. Denck and Hut called for a conference of Baptist preachers, and led a meeting of representatives from 60 churches located in south Germany and Switzerland. Baptists in Strasbourg gained such influence that, for a time, religious liberty was practiced in the city. Here John Calvin found refuge and often studied and debated with the Baptist preachers. He married the widow of a Baptist preacher. Unfortunately, he did not accept most of the Baptist distinctives, and he later played a part in the persecution of Baptists in Switzerland.

Hans Denck died from a local plague in 1528 at only 32 years of age. In only four years, he had proved to be an incredible church builder, leading in the establishment and growth of two large churches. In the year of Denck's death, Hans Leupold, who took Denck's place as the bishop (or senior pastor) of the Augsburg church, was arrested at a prayer meeting. Eighty-seven others were arrested with him. In prison, he wrote several hymns that expressed his love and devotion to Christ and the Word. After a local trial, he was beheaded and five other church leaders were also killed. Every known church member was branded with a hot iron, and others were also whipped and ordered out of town with the threat of death if they returned. By 1530, there was no longer a Baptist church meeting in Augsburg.

Persecution spread, and in 1528, the pastor and 70 members of the Baptist church in Rottenburg were beheaded and their bodies burned. Their pastor, Leonard Scheimer, had been a former Roman Catholic priest, as had the pastor of the Baptist church in Schwartz. The Schwartz pastor's trial record shows that he was clearly a Baptist in the sense of teaching all of the Baptist distinctives. His belief in Bible truth cost him his head. At Salzburg, 18 Baptists were burned at the stake, and 70 Baptists, including two pastors, were executed in Lintz. Baptists became known as "Garden Brethren" from their practice of meeting by night in gardens and isolated solitary places.

In Worms, the Baptists grew greatly in popularity and influence. The Lutheran pastor, Jacob Kautz, became convinced of the Baptist doctrines and identified with them. His successor at the Lutheran Church also became a Baptist. He is remembered only by the name, "Hilarious." The preachers were ordered out of town by the city council, but they refused to leave. The local authorities were afraid to arrest them because the preachers were so popular with the local population. A large Baptist church continued with relatively little persecution in Worms for several years. Persecution spread to the previously safe town of Strasbourg. The pastor there, Pilgrim Marbeck, was imprisoned and wrote a tremendous defense of the separation of church and state. His writing is still one of the most quoted on separation of church and state. Marbeck, a former Catholic priest, was released from prison, but banished from Strasbourg. He moved to Augsburg where he soon died. The cause of his death is debated.

It is important to note that some of these persecutions came from authorities who acknowledged the Roman Catholic Church, others from those who recognized Lutheran leadership. Both Lutheran and Roman Catholic leaders took the same position with respect to dealing with Baptists and others who taught religious liberty. In 1529, Charles V, Emperor of Germany, dealt with the rise of the Anabaptists. His edict following the church council at Spires reads in part:

> . . . *clearly ordained that all and every Anabaptist, or rebaptized person, whether male or female, being of ripe years and understanding, should be deprived of life, and, according to the circumstances of the individual, be put to death by fire, sword, or otherwise; and whenever found should be brought to justice, indicted, and convicted; and be no otherwise judged, tried, or dealt with, under pain of heavy and severe punishment.*

The results of this decree led to the deaths of thousands of Baptists; however, the movement continued to spread. In many German states there was massive persecution of Anabaptists. However, some German Princes defied the orders of the Emperor. The ruler of the region of Hesse is remembered as Philip the Magnanimous or Philip of Hesse. He refused to go along with any kind of religious persecution, and he protected the Anabaptists and other non-conformists in his state. He eloquently defended religious freedoms, but his attempts to defy the Emperor were relatively futile. He was imprisoned and, eventually, was forced to cooperate with Charles V. However, Hesse continued to remain a safer region for Anabaptists than most of Germany. In Schwarzburg, the local ruler, Count Gunther, protected the Baptists at the risk of his own life. He was fortunately successful.

Baptists were also protected in the German town of Wassenburg by a local ruler named Werner von Pallant. Under the leadership of Johannes Campanus, a local preacher, the church in Wassenburg determined to use their freedom as a base for sending missionaries throughout Germany. This so angered Melanchthon, Martin Luther's chief assistant, that he pressed for persecution of the Baptists in the region. Campanus was arrested and spent 20 years in prison, dying there. Most of the missionaries ordained by his church were also executed. Hubmaier was arrested and burned at the stake. Three days later his wife was drowned.

In many German towns, the Anabaptists were so popular that local authorities were careful about how they carried out their persecutions. Throughout this period, for example, there was a large Baptist church in Cologne, Germany. This church was constantly harassed, but it escaped the violent persecutions that so many Baptist churches had to undergo.

Four major controversies from this period involved the Baptists.

- The first had to do with Thomas Munzer and the Peasants' Revolt.

Munzer had been a Roman Catholic priest before his conversion. He became a Lutheran pastor and received his first pastorate at the direct recommendation of Martin Luther. Munzer eventually broke with the Lutherans over his teaching of separation of church and state. He led the peasants in demanding political, economic, and religious freedom. His views were remarkably similar to those of the founders of the American Republic. Unfortunately, he did not have the great military leaders in his movement that we saw involved in the American War for Independence. His armies were quickly and totally crushed.

Munzer is often called an Anabaptist because of his fervent devotion to the idea of religious liberty. He was not a Baptist, however, because he continued to teach the baptism of infants by sprinkling. He met with a group of Swiss and German Baptists who refused to endorse his rebellion. Some did not feel that violent rebellion was ever justified. Others believed that the time was not right and that the rebellion had no chance of success. Many Anabaptists, however, fought in Munzer's armies. However ill-conceived Munzer's timing and military leadership were, he should be remembered as a friend of freedom. Had he been successful, he undoubtedly would be remembered the same way that George Washington is today. The Anabaptists were such zealous advocates of religious liberty that the name Anabaptist soon was applied to all who stood for separation of church and state.

- Another controversial figure from this period was Melchoir Hoffman.

Hoffman was a former Lutheran preacher who was identified with the Anabaptists because he immersed only believers. He was not a complete Baptist, however, because he did not accept the sole authority of Scripture. He believed that he was continuing to receive revelations from God, and he prophesied the end of the world for 1533. In 1533, he returned to Strasbourg in defiance of city authorities to await the Second Coming. He was arrested and spent the next ten years in prison, dying there in 1543.

- Another important controversy involved Baptist preacher, Hans Hut.

Hut extended his teaching of separation of church and state to a teaching of the separation of individual Christians and the state. He spoke against military service, paying taxes to the German state, and recognition of the civil government as ordained by God. It is easy to understand his perspective when you remember the times in which he lived. Armies were being used to persecute Christians, taxes made it financially possible, and civil government had so rebelled against God that it had become the agent of religious persecution. However, most Baptists rejected Hut's approach. His teaching was often used by various rulers as grounds for persecuting all Baptists. Hut was killed in Augsburg while trying to escape from prison.

- The most famous controversy of this period had to do with the "Kingdom of Munster."

An itinerant preacher, Jan Matthys, who had been a follower of Melchoir Hoffman, claimed revelation from God. He led his followers to control of the German city of Munster. They defied the government of Germany and declared that they were establishing the "New Jerusalem." A Communist economic system was established by John Leyden who taught separation of church and state. Leyden attracted many Anabaptists to Munster by promising them religious freedom. He taught polygamy and finally claimed to personally be the Messiah. Munster was finally surrounded by an army composed of both Roman Catholics and Lutherans. After a brutal siege, the city was captured and the "New Jerusalem" leaders were executed. Because so many Anabaptists participated in the defense of Munster, the Anabaptists have often been blamed for the excesses of Matthys and Leyden. It should be remembered, however, that both men were ordained Lutheran preachers and both practiced infant baptism. They also denied sole authority of Scripture.

The end of the Reformation period in Germany saw the

Anabaptist movement outlawed and persecuted, but growing in strength and influence.

Chapter 23

Baptists in Holland

"Wherefore let them that suffer according to the will of God commit the keeping of their souls to him in well doing, as unto a faithful Creator" (1 Peter 4:19).

By 1525, many German Anabaptists had fled to Holland and, while it was ruled by Charles V, there was also great opposition to his rule. Local leaders often defied his edicts, and non-conformists hoped to gain refuge from persecution there. Many Baptist churches were started there, and the movement grew quickly. However, persecution soon followed. In 1527, a widow named Weynken Claes was strangled, and her body was burned at the stake. Her crime was having been rebaptized in a Baptist church. Three other Baptists were burned at the stake that year; however, the movement continued to grow. By 1533, over a thousand baptisms had taken place in the town of Emden alone.

In 1531, Sicke Freerks, the town tailor at Leeuwarden, was arrested for being a Baptist. During his lengthy trial, the issues of salvation and baptism were clearly discussed. This made a profound impression on a very young Roman Catholic priest named Menno Simons. The courage of Sicke Freerks drove Menno to study the New Testament, and he was converted. For five years, he continued as a Roman Catholic priest, but he finally identified himself with the Baptists. Freerks was tortured and executed, but his testimony had led to the conversion of this man who would become one of the most influential Baptist preachers.

Many more Baptists were executed during the fourth decade of the Sixteenth Century. In 1535, the punishment of being burned at the stake was decreed for all Baptists. This was confirmed in 1540 and again in 1550. These measures could not destroy the Baptist movement. One Baptist pastor, Leonard Bouwens, left written records of over 10,000 converts whom he baptized. As the wave of persecution spread, Menno Simons became increasingly uncomfortable as a Roman Catholic priest. His study of Scripture had led him to accept the Baptist distinctives. His personal salvation caused his heart to go out to his persecuted brethren so, in 1536, he left the priesthood and was baptized upon his profession of faith in Christ. He accepted the pastorate of the Baptist church at Groningen and spent a peaceful four years as pastor there.

In 1541, he became the pastor of a Baptist church in Amsterdam, but he spent the next 18 years as a fugitive with a price put on his head by Roman Catholic leaders. He traveled throughout Holland and Germany, never staying very long in one place. He founded many small churches during his travels. A large financial reward was offered for information leading to his arrest, and any Baptist who turned him in was offered a complete pardon. There were several attempts to betray him, but he always escaped.

Some of his associates were not so fortunate. Tjaert Reynerson, a farmer, was beheaded because he had allowed Menno to hide at his farm. Ian Ceaeson was beheaded for writing an introduction to a book written by Menno Simons. Simons' books were outlawed, and the death penalty was instituted for being found with a book written by him.

Simons and his followers found refuge in 1553 when the Lord of Fresenburg, a powerful Dutch noble, invited the Baptists to move into his region and live under his protection. Thousands of Baptists moved to his region, often founding their own villages. Here, Simons lived in peace for his last eight years.

Menno Simons wrote many books and pamphlets, clearly teaching all the Baptist distinctives. But his followers made a great issue of another distinctive that most Baptists refused to accept. Menno and his followers taught pacifism — the belief that violence, even in self-defense, was never justified. The Baptists who accepted this idea were usually called Mennonites, in honor of their most famous teacher. During the life of Menno, and for several decades after, Baptists and Mennonites were usually in close fellowship. They respected each others' baptism and ordination. Baptists preached in churches called Mennonite, and Mennonites considered themselves a branch of the Baptist movement. However, disputes over pacifism and the growing Mennonite emphasis on works for salvation split the two groups. By the Eighteenth Century, the Mennonite churches no longer practiced baptism by immersion of believers only and were no longer considered part of the Baptist movement.

The Prince of the Dutch state of Orange, William, determined to destroy the rule of Philip II of Spain over Holland. Philip had "inherited" Holland from his father, Charles V, who was a tyrant in every respect, denying economic, political, and religious freedom to his people. He is the one who formed the Spanish Armada to conquer England. William of Orange united Protestants, Baptists, and other non-conformists into an army to break Catholic power. Again and again he led his troops against vastly larger Catholic armies and finally achieved independence for Holland. He was immediately put under pressure to establish a Calvinist (Reformed) state church and turn on his former Baptist allies. When faced with similar pressure, Zwingli renounced his earlier views and turned against his former Baptist friends. But William was no Zwingli.

As the new nation of Holland was formed, it was decreed that "every individual should remain free in his religion, and that no man should be molested or questioned on the subject of divine worship." William was sometimes known as William the Silent because of his shrewd ability as a diplomat. He had been a Lutheran but had attended a Catholic school. As an adult he personally attended a Calvinist church. He had refused to carry out the orders of Charles V concerning religious persecution, and he had convinced Charles V to leave him alone. For all of his varied religious background, he is the one who created a safe refuge for Baptists during the Sixteenth Century. Baptists from all over Europe fled to Holland for safety. William was assassinated by a Roman Catholic agent, but his son, Prince Maurice, continued his struggle for liberty. A descendant of his, William III of Orange, brought religious freedom to England when he became King of England.

Baptists flourished in Holland. Even Rembrandt, the famous painter, was associated with a Baptist church in Holland. He painted many portraits of preachers, including several Baptists. Rembrandt was a zealous advocate of religious and political liberty, and this is communicated in several of his paintings. Several famous doctors and inventors were numbered among the Baptists of Holland, including the inventor of street lights and the prototype of the horse-drawn fire engine, J. Van der Hayden.

The German preacher, Kasper Schwenkfeld, had a great impact on both German and Dutch churches. He is often thought of in connection with the Baptists because of his great emphasis on personal salvation, baptism by immersion, and separation of church and state. Originally one of Luther's friends and followers, his doctrinal convictions caused him to be forced out of Germany. His preaching and writing in Holland helped to pave the way for religious freedom there. His Biblical teaching about baptism helped to open the door for many Baptists in Holland. Although Schwenkfeld never identified with the Baptists, he often fellowshipped with them. He and the Baptists were both conscious of an important difference between them. He taught that Scripture was the final authority, but that there was continuing personal revelation from the Holy Spirit. The Baptists taught that the Scriptures were the only revelation from God. His followers later were among the first group to settle in the Pennsylvania colony on the eastern seaboard in America. They still have many churches in Pennsylvania today.

Another Dutch preacher often remembered in connection with the Anabaptists is David Joris. He was well known for his teaching about separation of church and state and believers' baptism. However, he was not a complete Baptist because he believed that he was continuing to receive revelations from the Lord. He taught that the Millennium was to begin in his lifetime. After several of his followers had been executed, including his mother, he went into hiding. After his death, his body was dug up and burned by his enemies.

Another preacher who travelled back and forth between Germany and Holland was Jacob Huter. He was a strong Baptist who greatly emphasized the voluntary sharing of goods among Christians. He and more than a thousand of his followers were executed. The survivors gathered in Holland after religious freedom was established there. The Hutterrte Brethren are descended from this group. In the Eighteenth Century, most of the Hutterrte Brethren moved to Russia where they flourished until the rise of Communism in the Twentieth Century.

Another group with a Dutch Anabaptist background are the Amish. Jacob Ammann was a Mennonite teacher with a very legalistic interpretation of separation from the world. He seems to have been genuinely Baptist in his own doctrine, but his followers quickly carried his doctrine of separation over to the doctrine of salvation. When they did that, they ceased to be evangelicals. Many of the Amish emigrated to the United States.

At times, the Dutch government wavered from the concept of religious liberty, but the days of violent persecution never returned. Throughout the latter half of the Sixteenth Century and the Seventeenth Century, Holland was the place of refuge for Baptists and other non-conformists throughout Europe. Baptists developed into the largest percentage of the general population in Holland. They continued to build Baptist churches and seminaries that influenced later generations for many years.

The separatist Pilgrims fled to Holland seeking religious freedom before moving on to the New World. Holland became the first modern country that developed around the Baptist idea of separation of church and state.

Many Baptists from many countries paid for their faithfulness with their lives. Their testimony to the sole authority of Scripture lives on.

Chapter 24

English Baptists

"And in nothing terrified by your adversaries: which is to them an evident token of perdition, but to you of salvation, and that of God. For unto you it is given in the behalf of Christ, not only to believe on him, but also to suffer for his sake" (Philippians 1:28-29).

Henry VIII energetically persecuted Baptists in England through each of his different religious phases. Early in his reign, Alice Grevill, a lady who testified to being a Baptist for 28 years, was executed in London, and several leaders from a Baptist church in London were also burned at the stake. Henry even sent troops to help with the persecution of Baptists in Germany. In 1533, he issued a decree that gave all people who believed in believers' baptism 12 days to leave the country, and many left England. Others continued openly, while still others were imprisoned. Some others were executed.

Even the evangelical part of the Church of England supported the persecution of Baptists. The famous evangelical leader, Hugh Latimer said, "The Anabaptists that were burnt in divers towns in England ... went to their death ... without any fear in the world, cheerfully. Well, let them go!" Three times — 1538, 1540, and 1550 — English kings issued Acts of Pardon. These Acts forgave all prisoners and convicts of the crimes for which they had been convicted, although some violent crimes were not included. Each time Baptists were specifically excluded. Jails were emptied of thieves, robbers, and vagabonds, but Baptists remained in prison.

Eventually, the death penalty was instituted for reading Baptist books. One Englishman, writing to Erasmus, joked that it was a wonder that firewood was not scarce because so many Baptists had been burned at the stake.

Many Dutch Baptist missionaries came to England during this period, and a number of them were executed. Baptists were known by several names:

- Anabaptists,
- Baptists,
- Lollards, and
- some students of church history even called them Donatists and Paulicians.

When Henry VIII died, his son, Edward VI, became king. He was sympathetic to religious freedom and eventually put an end to executions because of religious beliefs. Before he did so, however, at least two Baptists were executed. Joan of Kent was burned at the stake for smuggling Baptist books into the Royal Court. Edward put an end to such barbarity, but, unfortunately, he was always in poor health, and he died after ruling for only six years. He had no children, so he was followed to the throne by his sister, Mary.

Mary was a very intense Roman Catholic who had learned her Roman Catholicism from her mother, Catherine, Henry's first wife. She never forgot that England had become Protestant in connection with the abandonment of her mother by her father. She determined to bring England back to Roman Catholicism, and even married Philip II, the Roman Catholic King of Spain in order to strengthen the Roman Catholic claim to England.

Mary had almost all of the evangelical leadership of the Church of England burned at the stake. These professing Christians, who had been willing to send other believers to their death, now reaped what they had sown. Latimer, who could so unflinchingly send Baptists to the stake, now went to the stake himself. Baptists, meanwhile, fared no better under Mary, and many Baptist preachers were also burned at the stake. Mary died after ruling for only five years and is remembered as "Bloody Mary." Her death was greeted with rejoicing throughout England.

The next ruler of England was Mary's sister, Elizabeth, the daughter of Henry VIII and Anne Boleyn. She finally re-established the Protestant nature of the Church of England and, for a while as she reorganized the church, all persecution was suspended. Many thought this was a commitment to religious toleration, but they had misunderstood her motives. The Baptists began to operate much more openly, and many Baptists from the mainland of Europe sought refuge in England. This respite was only temporary, however. Elizabeth declared herself the supreme authority for the Church and demanded that nothing be preached against her will.

The Baptists had quickly grown into a strong and visible minority in England, but Elizabeth would take care of that. She established a commission with the responsibility to destroy the independent churches. Again, Baptists were burned at the stake in England.

Robert Browne, known as the "Father of the Congregationalists," became a prominent preacher in England during this time. He studied with some Dutch Baptists in Norwich, England. Browne became convinced of all the Baptist distinctives except believers' baptism, and his preaching led to the formation of many independent churches in England. These independent churches stood nobly for religious liberty and separation of church and state, even though it brought them severe persecution. Each of this new wave of independent churches decided for themselves about baptism. Some were Baptists, and some practiced infant baptism. They were often called Congregationalist Churches because of their emphasis on independent churches composed of believers who governed their own affairs. There was often fellowship between the Baptists and the early Congregationalists.

The difference between the Baptists and the evangelical

Protestants is made clear by the case of Bishop Hooper of the Church of England, who came to the conclusion that Scripture must be seen as the sole authority. Hooper began to preach that truth and asked the Church of England to conform its practices to that doctrine. He was rebuked and reminded that both the ruling Monarch and the Church leadership were also spiritual authorities. He was told to abandon his position of the sole authority of Scripture because such a position would logically lead to separation of church and state and even rule out infant baptism. He was ordered to stop such preaching or leave the Church of England and identify with the Baptists who had always stood for the sole authority of Scripture.

The persecution under Elizabeth was so severe that Baptists, Congregationalists, Quakers, and other independents began to flee to the forests and mountains again. After Elizabeth's death, her second cousin, King James of Scotland became the English King.

A large minority within the Church of England called for Scripture to be given a greater rule in the church and for evangelical doctrine to become the official doctrine of the church. These were called Puritans, and they followed the teachings of John Calvin.

Baptists continued to be oppressed in England; however, James turned away from the past policy of executions and turned to imprisonment and fines. Baptists appealed to James for religious freedom; however, it was not granted. But following their appeal, James seemed to lose interest in persecuting them. He did not stop various church leaders from persecuting the Baptists, but he did not participate as he had previously. Many Baptists fled to Holland, while others were permitted to participate in new English colonies on the Atlantic seaboard of North America.

In 1614, Mark Busher, a member of a Baptist church in England, wrote the first book published in England advocating religious liberty. He had to flee to Holland after it was published, though he was eventually able to return to England. His book greatly influenced John Milton and the political writer, John Locke. Locke's political writings greatly influenced people like Thomas Jefferson, George Washington, and James Madison. The Declaration of Independence is basically a restatement of Locke's political philosophy applied to the situation of the American colonies.

One of the most famous events of English Baptist history took place during this time. It is often called the "Se-Baptist Episode." John Smyth had been a Church of England preacher who became convinced of sole authority of Scripture and separation of church and state. He left the Church of England and returned to his home town of Gainsborough. In Gainsborough, there were two Congregationalist churches. One became the group from which most of the Pilgrim colonists to Plymouth Bay Colony came. Smyth became the pastor of the other church. Because of persecutions, the majority of the members of both churches fled to Holland and, while there, Smyth became convinced of the truth of believer's baptism. He led his congregation in the study of this doctrine, and they agreed. He baptized himself, and then most of the members of his congregation. Disputation arose over whether or not his baptism was legitimate, and he even began to question it. He presented himself to a Mennonite church for membership, and they would not recognize his self-baptism. It appears that he died while they were discussing how to handle the situation. Most of his church congregation applied for membership to the Mennonite church, and they were eventually admitted as members.

A small number of the congregation did not want to join the Mennonites. They were led by Thomas Helwys, who became their pastor and continued to accept John Smyth's baptism. He and his followers returned to England and formed a Baptist church where Helwys taught aggressively against the Calvinist doctrine of predestination of the Puritans. This doctrine was starting to find acceptance among many Baptists. Because of the fact that Helwys strongly taught a general atonement (that Christ had died for *all* men), his church became known as a General Baptist church. Soon, this name was applied to any Baptist church which taught a general atonement. Churches which taught that Christ died *only* for the elect became known as Particular Baptists. Helwys then attacked King James and was arrested and imprisoned. He died soon after.

It should be noted that historians sometimes differ on the details of the "Se-Baptist Episode" and the origin of the General and Particular Baptists. Some even deny that Smyth and Helwys were immersionists, but the evidence that they were legitimate Baptists is overwhelming (see John Christian's, *A History of the Baptists*).

An extremely well-known Baptist church arose during this time from an independent background. An independent church was founded by Henry Jacob in Southwark. He moved to the Virginia colony and was succeeded by John Lathrop who was imprisoned for his work. After being released, he led most of the church to New England. Those who remained in New England became known as the Jacob-Lathrop church. A portion of the church became convinced of Baptist principles and formed an independent Baptist church under the leadership of John Spillsbury; however, no one in the church had ever been baptized by immersion.

They sent one of their number, Richard Blunt, to Holland to be baptized by immersion by the Mennonites. He returned and baptized the other members of the church. William Kiffin, a member of the church, became well known as a leader of the Particular Baptists.

Chapter 25

Baptist Ideas Spread Throughout Europe

"For which cause we faint not; but though our outward man perish, yet the inward man is renewed day by day. For our light affliction, which is but for a moment, worketh for us a far more exceeding and eternal weight of glory; While we look not at the things which are seen, but at the things which are not seen: for the things which are seen are temporal; but the things which are not seen are eternal" (2 Corinthians 4:16-18).

Baptists were well represented in many European countries during, and immediately following, the Reformation. There are records of several Baptist churches in Italy during this period. These churches were vigorously persecuted by the Roman Catholic Church and local governments. A former Roman Catholic priest turned Baptist preacher, Julius Klampherer, was drowned in Venice in 1561. The pastor of the Baptist church in Venice, Franciscus Van Der Sach, along with one of his deacons, was drowned in 1564.

Many Italian Baptists fled to Moravia, others to Holland. Some stayed, and there is a report of a group of representatives of over 60 Anabaptist preachers meeting in northern Italy. One of the best known was Camillo Renato, an outspoken defender of believers' baptism. Another well-known Anabaptist from Italy was named Tiziano. The Italian Anabaptist movement became heavily influenced by those who denied the Trinity. While still advocating the separation of church and state and baptism by immersion, the

Italian Anabaptists became genuine heretics in the Biblical sense — they denied the deity of Christ.

Many of the followers of Hans Hut moved to Hungary. They were led by a Baptist preacher named Peter Weidman. They underwent great persecution. Many moved to Russia. Their descendants moved to the United States during the late 1800's.

The death penalty was proscribed for Baptists in Austria. King Ferdinand committed himself with devilish intensity to destroying the Baptists. Thousands were burned at the stake. Many were bound together by chains and cast into rivers. In Vienna, an entire Baptist congregation was arrested. The women and children were set free, but the able-bodied men were informed that they would be forced to serve as sailors. They attempted a mass escape and all but 15 succeeded. The 15 who were recaptured disappeared never to be heard from again.

Our information about Baptist ideas in Russia is very limited. It is known that the Paulicians, Waldenses, Bogomils, Taborites, Bohemian Brethren, Mennonites, and Amish were all represented in Russia. The number of Baptists in Russia seems relatively small until the rise of the Stundists in the Nineteenth Century. The Stundists, tracing their heritage to earlier Baptist groups in Russia, experienced great growth during the Nineteenth Century. This was a genuine Baptist group, numbering in the millions. This group was heavily persecuted following the Communist takeover but survives until this day. They have merged with other Baptistic groups as part of the Evangelical Christian Union. Their exact numbers are unclear, but they still seem to exist in the millions in Russia.

Baptists gained great prominence in Poland. During the Reformation, the concept of religious freedom came to temporary acceptance by the Polish monarchy and nobles. Many Italian and Swiss Baptists fled there and spread Baptist ideas to the people of Poland.

One of the first Polish Baptist leaders was Peter

Gonesius. He began a church which was to have great success in planting churches throughout the rest of Poland. Within 15 years, a meeting was held representing 47 Baptist churches. Gregory Paulus became a noted Baptist leader in Poland. He pastored a church in Cracow. Polish Baptists issued a 160-page catechism for the training of their children. This was produced by the church at Cracow.

Unfortunately, the Baptists of Poland came to be dominated by a heretical group later known as the Socinians. Their teachers believed in what we call the Baptist distinctives, but they denied one of the most basic fundamentals of the faith — the deity of Christ. This doctrine became so widely accepted among Polish Baptists that there is almost no record of Baptists in Poland who were doctrinally sound after 1570. Faustus Socinius was a teacher who was especially successful and who became identified in the minds of many with this heresy.

In Lithuania, a well-known pastor of a large independent church, John Caper, Sr., became convinced of believers' baptism. He was baptized by immersion and openly identified with Baptists. He was later drowned by a group of local hoodlums in the same pool in which he had been baptized.

During the Seventeenth and Eighteenth Centuries, the Baptist witness in Europe, outside of England and Holland where it was very strong, seems to have been very limited. Here and there, brave individuals and isolated churches took a lonely stand for Bible truth. During the Nineteenth Century, however, the Baptist witness grew swiftly throughout western Europe.

In 1810, in French Flanders, a farmer found a Bible. He and his neighbors read it, studied it, and were led in 1819 to form an independent church. They practiced believers' baptism. A young Frenchman who had been converted in Scotland, Henry Pyt, became their pastor. He clearly taught all of the Baptist distinctives. In 1831, an American Baptist pastor vacationing in France became burdened for the country. Upon his return, he influenced the sending of several missionaries to France. These missionaries worked with Pyt to build churches. For several years they were harassed by local government, but in 1848 religious freedom came to France. During the Nineteenth Century, these efforts resulted in starting at least 30 churches in France and in sending missionaries to Switzerland and Belgium.

The great hero of the Baptist movement in Germany during the Nineteenth Century was undoubtedly Johann Oncken. Oncken was a Lutheran who had the chance to travel throughout Europe from the age of 13 until he was 21. He became acquainted with an independent church in London, England, and he was converted there. He became an independent missionary to Hamburg, Germany, where he began a program of street preaching, book distribution, Sunday schools, and home meetings that attracted a large following in Hamburg. He began to study the subject of baptism, and he contacted the British Baptists for more information. He became convinced of believers' baptism, and he was baptized by a Professor Sears, a Bible teacher at an American Baptist college who was traveling in France. Oncken had endured a great amount of persecution as an independent, and he experienced even more as a Baptist. He was imprisoned, fined, and his church services were dispersed by the military. When his situation attracted a great amount of attention in England and the United States, the local persecution was relaxed. Oncken ministered in Hamburg for a total of 59 years.

This Baptist church in Hamburg became one of the greatest missionary churches of all time. Within 11 years, they had started 26 churches throughout Germany. In 1848, official religious toleration was granted. Oncken led the German Baptists in forming a missionary association and beginning a seminary in Hamburg. The church in Hamburg sent missionaries to Sweden, Denmark, Russia, and virtually every country of Europe. It is estimated that literally hundreds of Baptist churches resulted from these endeavors. The church in Hamburg and most of the churches associated with it were eventually destroyed during World War II. Many of the pastors had previously been executed by Adolf Hitler for defying his government.

In 1843, two Swedish seamen became acquainted with Baptists in New York City. One presented himself for believers' baptism and ended up staying in the United States. The other, F. O. Nilson, returned to Sweden and eventually went to Oncken's church in Hamburg for further study. He eventually presented himself for believers' baptism and became a missionary to Sweden. After three years, Nilson was banished from Sweden. He then pastored for two years in Denmark. Then he led a group of Swedish Baptists to the United States where they could have religious freedom. After seven years, he was allowed to return to Sweden, and he began a Baptist church in Gothenburg. Missionary pastors from Hamburg began a church in Stockholm, the capital of Sweden. By 1861, there were 125 reported Baptist churches in Sweden. Government persecution gradually faded in Sweden, and Baptists became the largest of the non-Lutheran groups in Sweden.

In 1860, a Baptist church was organized by Frederik L. Rymker in Norway. It was originally composed of seven members. Rymker was a Danish sailor who had been saved and baptized while in the United States. By 1877, there were 14 Baptist churches in Norway. The number of Baptist churches in Norway has never been large, but the number has continued to grow until the present.

In 1839, a Baptist church was organized in Copenhagen, Denmark, from people who had been won to Christ during a mission from Oncken's church in Hamburg. Its first pastor was imprisoned, and his place was taken by his brother who was also imprisoned. Persecution continued until 1850 when religious liberty was granted in Denmark. Baptist growth in Denmark remained limited.

In 1884, some evangelicals in Estonia were convinced of the truth of believers' baptism and were baptized by a German Baptist pastor. Most of them eventually had to flee to Sweden. In Latvia, Baptist churches were started by German Baptists.

It was not until the Twentieth Century that Baptist churches were started in most eastern European countries.

Chapter 26

Further Developments Among English Baptists

"*For this is thankworthy, if a man for conscience toward God endure grief, suffering wrongfully. For what glory is it, if, when ye be buffeted for your faults, ye shall take it patiently? but if, when ye do well, and suffer for it, ye take it patiently, this is acceptable with God*" (1 Peter 2:19-20).

The controversy between the General and Particular Baptists dominated Baptist affairs among the English during the second half of the Seventeenth Century. William Kiffin led the Particular Baptists in forming clear doctrinal statements and in making public "Confessions of Faith." Most General Baptists adopted all of the doctrinal principles of Arminianism, including the belief that believers could lose their salvation. Particular Baptists remained heavily influenced by Calvinism. Many Baptists refused to associate with either group feeling that both groups were too influenced by man-made doctrinal systems. Those people were called Regular Baptists.

Henry D'Anvers, a government official and military leader, became a Baptist and wrote a book on baptism which was widely circulated by Baptists.

The issue of fellowship with evangelical, non-Baptists became an issue among Baptists. Spillsbury and Kiffin split over this issue with Kiffin starting a church which only fellowshipped with other Baptists. Spillsbury then moved to the American colonies.

An unusually named character of this period was Praise

God Barbon, an independent preacher and member of the Parliament. He was such a prominent political leader that the famous "Long Parliament" in which he served is also called the "Praise God Barbon Parliament." At first he was an extreme opponent of the Baptists, but he later became convinced they were correct and identified himself with the Baptist movement.

King James I was succeeded by his son, Charles I, who was a strong advocate of the "Divine Right of Kings" — unlimited rule of a king as the will of God. Charles persecuted all dissenters, independents, and even the Puritans within the established church. Many Baptists fled to Holland, others to the American colonies. Strict laws were passed against all Anabaptists, Congregationalists, Quakers, and other independents. Samuel Howe, a Baptist pastor, was refused burial in a cemetery when he died because he was a Baptist, and his family was forced to bury him in a local road. A famous book written against the Baptists during this period was entitled *The Dippers Dipt*. It was full of extreme language and false accusations directed against the Baptists. All preachers who were not licensed by the Church of England were forbidden to preach during this time. John Milton, famous author of *Paradise Lost, Paradise Regained*, compared the new Church of England with the old Roman Catholic Church. One of his most famous quotes was, "New Presbyters but old Priest writ large."

A Baptist pastor named Samuel Oates was actually tried for murder because he baptized by immersion! A young lady whom he had baptized had died several weeks after her baptism, and the authorities decided that her immersion had caused her death. Oates was put on trial for her "murder." Several witnesses testified that she was in good health for several weeks after her baptism, and Oates was eventually found not guilty.

The dictatorial manner of Charles I finally pushed the English into open rebellion against him, and two civil wars were fought. After the second war Charles was overthrown, arrested, and beheaded. Oliver Cromwell, a military and political leader with strong Puritan leanings, became the virtual dictator — officially titled "Lord Protector" — of England. Many Baptists had supported Cromwell, and some of his generals were Baptists. He stood for religious liberty, and he resisted the attempts of his Puritan associates to persecute the Baptists. As the period referred to as the "Protectorate" continued, Cromwell finally gave in to the pressure to allow harassment of the Baptists, but he never allowed the violent persecutions of the past. He even wrote letters defending individual Baptists. During his government, the Baptists grew and prospered to an incredible degree.

A radical group known as the Fifth Monarchy Men arose during this time. Their most prominent leaders were a Baptist general, Thomas Harrison, and an independent preacher, Thomas Venner. They were "post-millennialists," believing that they could bring about the return of Christ and the Millennium by establishing the right government. Some Baptists supported the Fifth Monarchy movement, while others openly opposed it. This movement was eventually crushed militarily by Charles II. The involvement of Baptists in this violent group later was used as an excuse for persecuting Baptists.

After the death of Cromwell, his son could not keep his government together. Faced with anarchy, the English restored the son of Charles I, Charles II, to the throne. Before the restoration, Charles had given his word to support religious freedom, but he soon broke his word, persecuting all non-conformists as well as the Puritan element within the established church. Many Baptists were imprisoned and fined, but none were officially executed for being Baptists. However, several Baptist preachers were executed for other charges that seemed very suspect. All clergy who taught the sole authority of Scripture were expelled from the Church of England.

Benjamin Keach, a Baptist pastor, wrote a book for children explaining Baptist principles to them. He was arrested, his books confiscated and burned. He was placed in stocks, and a local mob was permitted to pelt him with garbage and refuse.

Charles appointed William Laud as the head of the Church of England. Laud's claim to fame was his hatred of Baptists. He is credited with making the statement, "I could be content to see an Anabaptist go to Hell on a Brownist's back." In 1641, Laud was convicted of high treason and removed from office. Persecution of Baptists continued, but it was more isolated and sporadic than it had been in the past. During this time the established English Church turned from its ancient practice of immersion (of infants) and began sprinkling. By 1648, immersion of anyone was outlawed!

After the death of Charles II, his brother, James II, became the ruling monarch. Daniel Defoe, author of the famous novel, *Robinson Crusoe*, identified with the Baptists. He also wrote in defense of religious freedom and was twice arrested for his writings. Under James II, the same general treatment of Baptists continued, and the Baptists opposed his attempt to reunite the Church of England with the Roman Catholic Church. He was soon opposed by a violent revolution, but the revolt was crushed and many, including the two grandsons of William Kiffin, were arrested and scheduled for execution. The aged Kiffin managed to get an audience with the king, and he pleaded for their lives without success.

One of the most famous of all Baptists lived during this period — John Bunyan. Bunyan preferred to call himself an independent, but it is clear that he taught all the Baptist distinctives. He was arrested three times for preaching without being licensed by the Church of England and those arrests led to a total of over 12 years in prison. While in prison, he wrote the Christian classic, *The Pilgrim's Progress*, as well as many other books. *The Pilgrim's Progress* has been the most highly regarded Christian book ever written (apart from the Bible, of course). Bunyan was finally released from prison and continued several years as a very popular preacher. Both Charles II and James II took note of his popularity. He died only three months before religious freedom came to England.

Finally, the English people overthrew James II in what is remembered as the "Glorious" or "Bloodless Revolution." James had such little support that he had to flee to France for his safety. The English appealed to William III, King of Holland, to become their new king. William was married to a member of the English royal family — Mary. He was also descended from William the Silent and Maurice. He held their same views of liberty and religious freedom, and he quickly established relative religious freedom in England. The days of fines and imprisonment were over.

Baptists grew greatly in this new, free atmosphere in England and, in 1717, the first Baptist college was opened in England. Dr. John Gill became a famous Baptist theologian and a spokesman for the Particular Baptist cause. The Stennett family was particularly important among English Baptists. Edward Stennett pastored a Baptist church in London and was followed by his son, Joseph. Both were active writers. Joseph's son, Samuel, followed his father and grandfather in the pastorate of the same church, and he became a spokesman for the Baptist cause.

By the middle of the Nineteenth Century, there were over 2,400 Baptist churches in Britain. There were a number of Regular Baptist publications and at least 11 Baptist colleges. Most Baptist churches had united for the purpose of promoting missions, and this organization was called the Baptist Union.

The period of revival known as the Great Awakening had a great effect on English Baptists, but the most influential preachers of the Great Awakening were John Wesley, the Arminian founder of the Methodists, and George Whitefield, an independent Calvinist. Many of the converts of the Great Awakening joined Baptist churches, and the many new Baptist churches were not always well received by the older established groups. A new fellowship of Baptists, usually called New Connection Baptists, was formed under the leadership of Dan Taylor.

Perhaps the most famous English Baptist was Charles Haddon Spurgeon, whose father and grandfather had been independent preachers. Spurgeon had been saved as a youth in a Methodist church, and his own study of the Scriptures convinced him of the reality of the Baptist distinctives.

Spurgeon built a huge church in London, easily the largest church in the world during that time. He became a national figure in England, and his sermons and comments were printed in newspapers around the world. He started his own college for the purpose of training preachers. Spurgeon's glory days — when people had to arrive early to get a seat at his church — are usually what are most remembered about Spurgeon; however, there is another very important side to his ministry that reveals his character and principled position.

By the time Spurgeon became prominent, there were growing doctrinal differences among the pastors in the Baptist Union. Some leading English Baptists were denying the inerrancy of Scripture, while others taught universalism — the idea that eventually everyone would be saved. Spurgeon openly fought against those heresies and identified the false teachers by name. This is often called the "Downgrade Controversy." After the Baptist Union failed to take a clear stand on these issues, Spurgeon withdrew from the group, and representatives of the Baptist Union later voted 2,050 to 7 to condemn him as divisive. Spurgeon's own brother, James, presented the motion. While Spurgeon remained the most prominent preacher in England, his popularity suffered, and he was never again very far from controversy.

Spurgeon's concern about the Baptist Union proved to be realistic. Within 50 years of the Downgrade Controversy, modernism had completely taken over the English Baptist movement. Today, there are very few English Baptists who still hold to the fundamentals of the Christian faith and the

Baptist distinctives. Modernism accomplished what centuries of state persecution had been unable to do. It virtually silenced the Baptist witness in England.

Chapter 27

Baptists in the American Colonies and on the Frontier

"*Blessed are they which are persecuted for righteousness' sake: for theirs is the kingdom of heaven. Blessed are ye, when men shall revile you, and persecute you, and shall say all manner of evil against you falsely, for my sake. Rejoice, and be exceeding glad: for great is your reward in heaven: for so persecuted they the prophets which were before you*" (*Matthew* 5:10-12).

The famous Pilgrims espoused many Baptist ideas even though they were not Baptists. They taught the sole authority of Scripture, the priesthood of believers, separation of church and state, soul liberty, independent churches, and the concept of a regenerated church membership. They came to the New World for the express purpose of being free to worship as they chose, and they endured the hardships of the wilderness for an opportunity to practice religious freedom. They were willing to pay the price in order to obey the Lord.

The area in which the Pilgrims were not Baptists was their understanding of the doctrine of baptism. Most of them accepted the ideas of infant baptism and sprinkling. From the Pilgrims, however, came a number of people whose study of the Scriptures led them to become Baptists. Francis Cooke, one of the original passengers on the *Mayflower*, became a Baptist preacher. This was after the establishment of a Baptist colony in Rhode Island. Cooke moved to the Dartmouth area, and started a Baptist church. The Pilgrims upheld his religious liberty, and several of them joined his church. Soon there were a number of Baptists among the areas that the Pilgrims settled.

As the Puritans settled all around the Pilgrims, they brought their ideas of a state church with them, and they soon began to harass the Baptists and other non-conformists. The independent English preacher, Roger Williams, fled the persecution of William Laud and came to the village of Salem, Massachusetts, where he became pastor of the church there. Two of his teachings angered the Puritans. First, he taught the complete separation of church and state and, secondly, he urged the conversion of the Indians. He was soon banished from New England.

Williams gained permission from Charles II to establish a colony where religious freedom would be guaranteed to everyone. This became the Rhode Island Colony. This was really an experiment on the part of Charles II.

A settlement was begun at Providence upon land purchased from the Indians. A number of Baptists fled there for personal safety, and Williams became convinced that their teaching on baptism was correct. He was baptized by one of them, and soon he baptized ten others; however, within three months he renounced his identification as a Baptist and became an independent again. He often said that Baptists were the closest to New Testament churches, but that no true New Testament church continued to exist.

Williams continued to promote the Rhode Island Colony and negotiate with both the English government and the Indians. He had more success with the Indians than any other colonial leader. He defended separation of church and state in many important publications. The Puritans wished to militarily destroy the Rhode Island Colony, but they could not because of the Royal Charter secured by Williams and maintained by the negotiations of Williams and John Clarke with the English government.

The first real continuing Baptist church in America was founded by John Clarke. He is often remembered as the father of American Baptists. He was both a leader in the Rhode Island Colony and a church builder and planter. Once, he and two other members of his church were visiting an aged church member who lived under the jurisdiction of the Massachusetts Bay Colony. The men were arrested and ordered to pay fines, but one of his members, Obadiah Holmes, refused to pay the fine and was publicly whipped. This caused Henry Dunster, first President of Harvard (the first American college), to study the Baptist positions. Dunster wanted to know why Holmes was willing to undergo persecution for the cause of believers' baptism. His study convinced him of the truth of believers' baptism. When he expressed this, he was dismissed from Harvard.

Obadiah Holmes later succeeded John Clarke as pastor of the Baptist church in Newport, Rhode Island.

The influence of Williams and Clarke created a colony where all men could worship as they pleased, and there were many Baptist churches in the colony; however, many religious groups were represented. One historian wrote, "Notwithstanding so many differences, here are fewer quarrels about religion than elsewhere, the people living peaceably with their neighbors of whatever profession."

Despite the persecutions awaiting them, the Baptists continued to increase in the Massachusetts Bay Colony. Welsh Baptists moved to the New World and began Welsh-speaking Baptist churches in both Massachusetts and Rhode Island. They were greatly influenced by a Welsh pastor named John Miles.

A Baptist church was begun in Boston in the home of the pastor, Thomas Gould, and persecution soon came. Various people were imprisoned for sympathizing with the Baptists, including the mother of David Yale, founder of Yale University.

The Puritans were unrelenting in their persecution of Baptists, Quakers, and other non-conformists. This was the time of the famous witchcraft trials. Various individuals in Salem were accused and punished as witches without there being any real evidence against them. Baptists opposed the witchcraft trials. Robert Calif, the pastor of the Baptist church in Boston, wrote a book against the foolishness of the trials, and the Puritans accused the Baptists of being defenders of the devil.

One important Puritan leader repented of persecuting the Baptists and openly spoke out for religious freedom. Cotton Mather, once a vicious persecutor, preached the ordination sermon for a Baptist in 1717. Unfortunately, very few Puritans agreed with him.

William Penn, whose father was a Baptist, founded the colony of Pennsylvania. Penn, a Quaker, was a supporter of religious liberty, and soon men of all religious persuasions flocked to the new colony. Baptists from England, Wales, Massachusetts, and Rhode Island soon moved to Pennsylvania and began churches there. Elias Keach, son of Benjamin Keach, came to Pennsylvania and became a leader among American Baptists. He eventually returned to London and became a pastor there. A group of Pennsylvania Quakers became convinced of believers' baptism and became known as Quaker Baptists.

A group of Germans who had become convinced of believers' baptism settled in New York and Pennsylvania. They were known as Dunkers or German Baptists.

Many Baptists also settled in the colony of New Jersey. They included Baptists from England, Holland, and Germany. Obadiah Holmes moved to New Jersey and pastored a Baptist church there. William Screven helped organize the first Baptist church in Maine, but persecution forced him and the other Maine Baptists to South Carolina. The early rulers of South Carolina determined to establish the Church of England by force but constantly met with resistance from the early settlers. Later governors were sympathetic to religious freedom (one was rumored to be secretly a Baptist), and they hesitated to enforce the concept of an established church.

There were Baptists among the original Dutch colonists

of New York, and English Baptists soon moved there after it was captured by the English.

There were few Baptists in the Southern colonies before the Great Awakening; however, some General Baptists had moved into Virginia. Baptist congregations were rare. Later, Baptists from Maryland and Wales moved into Virginia in great numbers.

Baptist churches in Philadelphia organized the Philadelphia Baptist Association that provided them a basis for cooperation in several projects. This idea of a voluntary association became very popular and was a common vehicle for Baptist churches to use in carrying out joint projects. Most colonial governments treated Baptists with hostility or outright persecution. Only in Rhode Island, Pennsylvania, and Delaware (and temporarily in New York, New Jersey, and Maryland) did they find the religious freedom and separation of church and state that was so important to them. In some colonies, the persecution became as great as it had been in England. Several New England Baptists formed the Warren Association, headquartered in Warren, Rhode Island, to campaign for religious freedom in the colonies. The Warren Association appointed Isaac Backus as its spokesman, and he traveled throughout the colonies campaigning for religious freedom and organizing aid for churches in trouble. He led the battle against paying taxes for the support of established churches, state licensure of preachers, and limitations upon publishing religious literature. While carrying out this work, Backus continued as the pastor of the same Baptist church for 60 years.

Baptists in Virginia found themselves in considerable conflict with the Church of England that was established by the colonial government. Baptists were ordered to pay taxes to the state church, but most refused. They were ordered to get licenses from the state or close their ministries, but most refused. Rewards were offered to anyone turning in a Baptist or Quaker. Children (infants) were taken from Baptist parents and baptized by force.

The Great Awakening led to a tremendous increase in the number of Baptists in Virginia: General, Regular, and Particular Baptists. Eventually the Regular and Particular Baptists merged, and a new group that was greatly influenced by the Great Awakening became popular. They were led by Samuel Stearns and were Arminian in doctrine, evangelistic in outlook, and quick to oppose the idea of formal Bible training for preachers. This Separate Baptist movement grew greatly in Virginia.

In 1768, three Baptists were arrested for witnessing in Virginia, and they continued to preach through the window of the Culpepper County jail. This attracted great crowds, and the authorities finally freed their prisoners rather than allow this to continue. This led to a tremendous upsurge in persecution. Baptists were constantly being fined for not attending the state church. Non-Baptists such as Patrick Henry, Thomas Jefferson, and James Madison came to their defense. The love of liberty that was about to be expressed in the War for Independence was outraged by this example of tyranny from the colonial government. Patrick Henry defended Baptists in court who were accused of preaching without a license, and he did it without cost to the preachers. His eloquence and his political influence usually led to acquittals. Jefferson and Madison campaigned for religious liberty in the state legislature; however, Baptists did not have freedom until after the War for Independence had been fought and won.

Baptists played prominent roles in the settlement of Kentucky. The famous explorer and settler, Daniel Boone, was a Baptist. In fact, the entire settlement at Boonesborough appears to have been Baptist. Squire Boone, Daniel's brother, was an ordained Baptist preacher who founded the first Baptist church in Kentucky. He later founded the first Baptist church in Indiana, near Squire Boone Caverns. Baptists were very widespread in Kentucky.

The first seminary in America was established by a Baptist church in New Jersey in 1756. A Baptist college was started in Rhode Island with the support of Baptists throughout the colonies.

Chapter 28

Baptists and the Foundation of the American Republic

❖❖❖

Biblical Basis for America's Three Branches of Government:
"For the LORD is our judge,
the LORD is our lawgiver,
the LORD is our king;
he will save us" (Isaiah 33:22).

❖❖❖

On May 4, 1776 (two months before the Declaration of Independence), the colony of Rhode Island officially withdrew from Great Britain and repudiated any allegiance to King George III. The large number of Baptists in this colony — which had been founded by Baptists — led the way in demanding freedom. Their doctrine of soul liberty logically led to the idea of personal freedom from the interference of government. Rhode Island had always been the most free of all the colonies. Rhode Island had no laws restricting religion, no taxation without representation, and no governor appointed by the king.

Rhode Island was quickly taken by British armies, but a strong local resistance tied down large numbers of British troops until the British government decided that occupying the colony was not worth the trouble.

Baptists were among the first groups to recognize the Continental Congress as the legitimate civil government for this new nation. Several associations of Baptist churches wrote letters of recognition to Congress that usually included an appeal to the Congress to remember that many of the former colonies did not yet have religious freedom. Baptists so completely supported the War for Independence that there is only record of one Baptist pastor siding with the British government. Even the Baptists of England supported the American patriots. Dr. Rippon, a well-known Baptist pastor in London, wrote the following to President Manning of Rhode Island College:

> *I believe all of our Baptist ministers in town, except two, and most of our brethren in the country were on the side of the Americans in the late dispute . . . We wept when the thirsty plains drank the blood of our departed heroes, and the shout of a king was among us when your well fought battles were crowned with victory; and to this hour we believe that the independence of America will, for a while, secure the liberty of this country, but if that continent had been reduced, Britain would not have long been free.*

The Baptist respect for religious and personal freedom meant more to the English Baptists than the desire to control the American colonies for financial gain.

Richard Furman, pastor of a Baptist church in Charleston, South Carolina, became a well-known spokesman against the British. He was chased out of Charleston by British agents, and he fled to the American military camp. The famous British general of that region, Lord Cornwallis, is quoted as having said that he "feared the prayers of that godly youth (Furman) more than the armies of Sumter and Marion." In fact, he offered a large financial bounty to anyone who would kill or capture Furman. Remembering this incident years later, President James Monroe would invite Furman to preach to the Congress and government leaders.

Many Baptist preachers served as chaplains in the patriot army, the most famous being John Gano. Gano had previously been one of two evangelists commissioned by the Philadelphia Association. The other evangelist was

Morgan Edwards, the only Baptist leader recorded as opposing the War for Independence.

Gano became a firm friend of George Washington, and it is said that their discussions convinced Washington of believers' baptism. There is a church record that Gano baptized Washington by immersion in front of 42 witnesses.

Many Baptist churches were devastated by the war such as Gano's church in New York that was used as a stable by the British calvary. Many Baptist churches were looted and destroyed.

John Hart of Hopewell, New Jersey, was a Baptist and a signer of the Declaration of Independence. He was forced to flee for his life and had most of his property and buildings destroyed. Of course, he had pledged everything to the cause of freedom when he signed the Declaration of Independence. He kept his word, even though it cost him everything.

After the war was over, the most crucial time came for our nation. It was a time of national development. Most revolutions that are fought for freedom end up failing during this period — usually leading to a worse government than the one that was overthrown. The attempt to create a Constitutional Democratic Republic was a unique answer to the question of civil government. For several years the adoption of the Constitution was hotly debated. In the North, the work of Baptists in Massachusetts is credited with securing the adoption of the Constitution in that state. Isaac Backus strenuously campaigned for the Constitution feeling that it presented the best chance for securing separation of church and state.

In Virginia, the battle over the adoption of the Constitution raged fiercely. Patrick Henry used all of his influence to oppose ratification of the Constitution because he did not believe that there were enough safeguards for liberty in the document. Baptists agreed, but they felt it was an important step in the right direction. John Leland of Culpepper County — a close friend of Thomas Jefferson — was the most prominent spokesman for the Baptists. In fact, Jefferson occasionally attended his church and credits Leland for influencing his philosophy of government. Leland led the Baptists of Virginia in supporting James Madison in his fight for the Constitution. The part Baptists played was so important that they were credited with making the difference in that pivotal state. Later, Baptists helped Madison get elected to the House of Representatives, and from that office Madison campaigned for the Bill of Rights, especially the First Amendment.

The First Amendment was demanded by all Baptists to secure their long-sought religious liberty. It guarantees: "Congress shall make no law respecting an establishment of religion or prohibiting the free exercise thereof." Baptists now had in writing what they had desired for so long — a guarantee of separation of church and state (national government).

The victory was only half won, however, since state governments were still free to make any laws respecting religion that they chose. This was addressed by the federal government with the passage of the Fourteenth Amendment following the Civil War. That Amendment declared that the states could not limit rights granted by the federal government.

Such states as Virginia, Massachusetts, and Connecticut still had powerful established churches and various forms of religious persecution. Opposition to the state church was powerful in all these colonies. In Virginia, an attempt to reach a compromise was made. Prominent Virginia politicians, including Patrick Henry, proposed recognizing four religious groups in the state — Episcopal (new name for the Church of England), Presbyterian, Baptist, and Methodist. Each citizen would be allowed to pay a tax to whichever one of those four churches he chose. This was vigorously supported by the Episcopal and Presbyterian churches, while the Methodists split over the issue. Baptists, however, fought vehemently against such a proposal.

Baptist goals did not include a government-sponsored advantage, but religious liberty. Thomas Jefferson and James Madison led the struggle for complete religious freedom. In 1785, they succeeded, and the Episcopal Church was no longer upheld and supported by the government. The Episcopal Church soon collapsed as its churches and clergy were no longer supported by tax money. The Episcopal Church ceased to be a major influence in Virginia.

Thomas Jefferson became a hated target of those who favored a state church. In his own religious beliefs, Jefferson denied the deity of Christ, personal salvation, and the inspiration of Scripture. In the minds of some, these beliefs motivated his opposition to the state church, and he was vigorously accused of trying to use the government to promote atheism and infidelity.

In their attacks against Jefferson, the Episcopal Church ignored the fact that he was a member in good standing of one of their own congregations. The Presbyterians joined in condemning Jefferson, but he found staunch political allies among the Baptists. He spoke to Baptist associations and received letters of support from Baptist churches. John Leland openly campaigned for his election to the Presidency. These unlikely allies were bound by a loyalty to individual liberty and the separation of church and state.

The battle for religious liberty was to be waged in Massachusetts for a long time. With Isaac Backus leading the way, Baptists fought against paying taxes to the state church and against the licensure of preachers. When the state, trying to avoid further conflict, offered to automatically license any ordained Baptist preacher, Backus still refused. Backus felt that he could not accept such licensure without acknowledging a power in man that should belong to God alone. The struggle in Massachusetts continued for a long time. Not until 1833 was complete religious liberty permitted there. The refusal of Baptists (and Quakers) to abandon their religious convictions is credited with finally forcing the state government to change.

George Washington is quoted as saying that Baptists were "throughout America, uniformly and almost unanimously, the firm friends to civil liberty and the persevering promoters of our Glorious Revolution." Without any doubt, the Baptists played a great role in securing independence and establishing liberty in our nation.

Chapter 29

Baptists Spread From Coast to Coast

"But the God of all grace, who hath called us unto his eternal glory by Christ Jesus, after that ye have suffered a while, make you perfect, stablish, strengthen, settle you. To him be glory and dominion for ever and ever. Amen" (1 Peter 5:10-11).

In the late 1700's, there were several attempts to unite Separate and Regular Baptists into fellowshipping associations. Some finally achieved this and began to call themselves United Baptists, while others continued to use the names Separate and Regular Baptists.

As the new country spread from coast to coast, the Baptist movement followed. After the War for Independence, Baptists, led by Hezekiah Smith and Morgan Edwards, started mission churches throughout New England. Isaac McCoy became a missionary to the Indians, and Luther Rice led the Baptists into forming a common foreign missions effort called the Missionary Baptist Convention.

Baptists formed an American Baptist Home Missionary Society for the purpose of starting churches on the frontier. Without a doubt, its most famous representative was John Peck, a former Congregationalist who had become convinced of the Baptist distinctives. In 1817, he was appointed a missionary to the area "west of the Mississippi." During his first 14 years he established over 30 churches, helped to build a Bible college in Illinois, and raised the finances for the Indian mission work of Isaac McCoy. Peck was not known as a great speaker, but he was considered a master or-

ganizer. He started churches and Christian schools throughout the western states. After 14 years his health broke, and
he was required to take a long rest. He returned to his work,
continuing to leave a trail of churches and schools behind
him.

Baptists were often found among the first pioneers in all
of the western regions.

- The first church in Kentucky was Baptist;
- This was also true in Indiana.
- The first non-French-Catholic Church in Illinois
  was Baptist.
- The first church in Cincinnati was Baptist.

The pastor of this church, John Smith, later got involved
in the conspiracy led by Aaron Burr to create a new nation
west of the Appalachian Mountains, and Smith was forced
to leave the area.

In New England, where Calvinism had been strong
among Baptists, an equally strong reaction developed. Under the leadership of Benjamin Randall, non-Calvinist Baptists formed a new association and termed themselves
Freewill Baptists. This movement quickly outgrew the Cal-
vinistic Baptists of New England and was soon sending missionaries to the West.

The Baptist Home Missions Society continued to look
westward, and one of its missionaries founded the First Baptist Church in Chicago. Its agents founded the first Baptist
churches in Indianapolis, St. Paul, Minneapolis, Omaha,
Denver, Portland, Los Angeles, Sacramento, and numerous
other cities west of the Appalachians. By 1832, there were
900 Baptist churches west of the Mississippi. Unfortunately, the Civil War and the controversies among the Baptists (see Chapter 31) slowed down the great influence of
this mighty force for church planting.

The event which has been termed the Second Great
Awakening (also called the Great Revival of 1800) had a
great influence on the Baptists, as well as other religious
groups. After the War for Independence, the spiritual life of

the nation declined greatly. Whiskey became virtually the national beverage (replacing tea), and Unitarianism became strong in the established denominations. Secret societies became an important part in the life of many Americans. Bibles were very expensive and difficult to obtain. John Peck declared that this scarcity of Bibles was the greatest difficulty in establishing sound churches in the West.

In 1800, a great revival broke out. Many churches were stirred and several denominations experienced great growth. This was especially true in the large eastern cities. In the West, camp meetings became very popular with large crowds gathering in tabernacles especially designed for such meetings. Preachers from several evangelical denominations would often preach. Baptists, Methodists, and Presbyterians often worked together in those meetings that were often very emotional. People swooned, went into convulsions, jerked from side to side, and often fainted. These extreme reactions caused many to feel that the revival was being corrupted, and many Baptists withdrew from the camp meetings.

Church attendance greatly increased around the country with many Baptist churches doubling or tripling their church membership. Historians still debate whether the influence of the camp meeting era and the Second Great Awakening was good or bad. Undoubtedly, some unfortunate things came out of this period, but its overall influence pointed many to the Bible and evangelical churches.

Baptists moved into the region that is now Florida, Mississippi, Louisiana, and Arkansas while that region was still under the control of Spain. The first Baptist church in Mississippi was started while the area was still under Spanish control. Richard Curtis, Sr., his sons, and several friends had moved into the area after the War for Independence. Most of these men had fought under the command of Francis Marion, the famous Swamp Fox. Their homes had been destroyed during the war, and they were looking for a new start. They started the Salem Baptist Church, even though they did not have a preacher available. They did have several converts, and the question arose over who should baptize those converts. They finally appointed one of their members to administer baptism.

A prominent Roman Catholic leader, Stephen DeAlva, was converted and baptized and joined the church, and this attracted the attention of the local authorities. Richard Curtis, Jr. (who had performed the baptism) was appointed preacher. He was ordered to quit teaching the Bible or he would be sent as a slave to the mines in Mexico. Curtis continued, and the Spanish Army served warrants for the arrest of Curtis, DeAlva, and another member of the church. They were forced to flee to South Carolina, but they returned three years later when the United States had taken control over the area. From Mississippi, Baptists spread throughout the former Roman Catholic regions.

The years before the Civil War are often referred to as the "years of Baptist expansion." The rest of the Nineteenth Century is referred to as the "years of Baptist education." In most areas, local associations of Baptists were formed to promote joint projects. On a state level, missionary conventions were formed, and these usually identified with either the Southern or Northern Baptist Conventions. Bible colleges, universities, seminaries, and publishing agencies became common. A national young people's organization was formed that reached thousands for Christ.

By 1850, it is estimated that one out of every 11 people identified with the Baptists. Only the Methodists had more influence. Baptists were no longer the outcasts of society or the objects of persecution, and Baptist schools were often attended by non-Baptists. Baptists could even run for public office. Sam Houston, first President of the Republic of Texas, and first Governor of Texas after it became a state, was an active Baptist.

The emphasis on colleges, nice campuses, and academic recognition seemed to change the character of the mainstream Baptist movement during this era. Rev. Thomas

Curtis of South Carolina said:

*The requisites for an institution of learning
are three B's: bucks, books, brains. Our brethren
usually begin at the wrong end of the three B's;
they spend all their money for bricks, have nothing to buy books, and must take such brains as
they can pick. But our brethren ought to begin at
the other end of the three B's.*

In an attempt to rectify this somewhat, Baptist leaders
put a greater emphasis on Bible training and seminary education. J. P. Boyce became a leader in this movement, and he
changed the way many thought about seminaries. He encouraged the admission of non-college graduates, practical
experience for students, and demanded a commitment from
all teachers to be loyal to the Baptist distinctives. He was
one of the founders of the Southern Baptist Theological
Seminary. During Boyce's lifetime, this seminary seemed
to inspire a return to basics among many Baptists.

One influential professor at Southern was John
Broadus, who had been a very successful pastor who now
devoted himself to teaching young men to preach. He encouraged the production of Sunday School literature, and
the first Southern Baptist publishing house was named
Broadman Press after him and another professor at Southern, Basil Manly, Jr. These men were devoted Baptists who
helped train many Baptist preachers.

One of the professors at Southern, Crawford Toy, a brilliant scholar, changed his view of Scripture and began to
question inerrancy. He was dismissed from the seminary in
what was one of the first conflicts over modernism in the
Baptist colleges. It surely was not to be the last conflict. The
battle between conservatives and theological liberals dominated the next 70 years of Baptist history.

The beginning of the Twentieth Century saw Baptists
active in every region of the country. They had enjoyed
freedom for almost a century and were as socially respect-
able as any other Christian group. They now comprised

about one-sixteenth of the American population. The American population had boomed because of millions of immigrants from Europe, and many of these people were of Roman Catholic or Lutheran background. Roman Catholicism was now the largest religious group in the nation, and Baptists comprised the second largest group.

Chapter 30

Baptists and the Modern Missionary Movement

"As they ministered to the Lord, and fasted, the Holy Ghost said, Separate me Barnabas and Saul for the work whereunto I have called them. And when they had fasted and prayed, and laid their hands on them, they sent them away" (Acts 13:2-3).

William Carey was born in 1761 in an Anglican home, but at age 17 he began to attend independent churches. Shortly thereafter he was converted to Christ, and, at age 21, he undertook his own study of infant baptism. He was determined to study the subject until he was sure of the Bible's teaching on the matter. The result was that he became convinced of believers' baptism and presented himself to Baptist pastor John Ryland for baptism. Carey soon opened a school, and became a Baptist pastor.

Carey was known for his unusual combination of great intellectual powers and his ability to be practical. He was a master of linguistic study, theology, history, and literature, although he was self-taught in all those areas. He is most remembered, however, for his missionary work.

Carey and some other Particular Baptist pastors were moved by the emphasis on missions and soul-winning that they saw among the Moravians. They began to preach on the need for missions in their local gatherings of preachers, and this preaching was met with a mixed reaction. Some vigorously opposed any attempt at missions because of their strong emphasis on predestination. Others recognized that

Scripture commanded evangelism, and they were determined to be obedient. Carey emphasized that they must be willing to "pray, plan, and pay."

Carey and John Thomas (a Baptist medical doctor) volunteered to become the first missionaries, while Pastor Andrew Fuller accepted responsibility of handling the finances for this first Baptist missions society.

For the rest of Andrew Fuller's life, he was viciously attacked for his efforts to raise money for missions. He became a very controversial figure among his own fellowship of Particular Baptists; however, the early missionaries testified repeatedly that without his efforts they would have been doomed to failure.

Carey and Thomas met with little visible success in the early years of their ministry in the nation of India. The Hindu people were not responsive to their message, and they were totally unfamiliar with the Scriptures. Poor health forced Thomas to England, but Carey was joined by William Ward and Joshua Marshman. They devoted their talents to translating the Bible into Bengali, a major Indian language. By 1801, they were distributing the New Testament in Bengalian. Carey eventually had a part in translating the Bible in 36 distinct languages, including every major language in India. Some people have called him the greatest linguist of all time.

Joshua Marshman wrote a poem to celebrate the publication of the Bengali New Testaments:

> Hail, precious Book divine!
> Illumined by thy rays,
> We rise from death and sin,
> And tune a Saviour's praise:
> The shades of error, dark as night,
> Vanish before thy radiant light!

Now shall the Hindus learn
The glories of our King:
Nor to blind gurus turn,
Nor idol praises sing;
Diffusing heavenly light around,
This Book their Shastras shall confound.

Deign, gracious Saviour, deign,
To smile upon Thy Word;
Let millions now obtain
Salvation from the Lord:
Nor let its growing conquests stay,
Till earth exult to own Thy sway.

The Baptist mission work in India, which had seen only one baptism in its first seven years, now began to flourish. Literally thousands were converted, and over 2,000 were baptized on one Sunday! One villager, Ram Krishnapur, was given one New Testament and three years later a number of the villagers presented themselves to Carey asking, "How may we obtain the fruits of Christ's death?" Several of the villagers had already believed, and a number were soon baptized. Several Hindu priests were converted and became Baptist preachers.

Carey had to endure many great hardships while serving Christ in India. Shortly after arriving in India, his wife became mentally ill and never recovered. In 1812, a fire destroyed the mission printing equipment and destroyed years of Carey's linguistic work. He simply did the work all over again.

After the death of Andrew Fuller, the missions society in England quit being a service agency to the missionaries and began demanding control over their activities, but Carey and his associates refused. He sent this message to the society: "We will never consent to put power over these premises and over ourselves into their hands, at a distance of a quarter of the globe's circumference ... We will carry on our work subject to no control but his (God's) most Holy Word."

Carey and his associates made such a positive impact on

India (during a time of great difficulty for the British Empire) that they were singled out for praise in the English Parliament.

In 1812, Adoniram Judson, an American Congregationalist missionary, sailed to India to begin an exciting and fruitful career of Christian service. He and his wife knew that they would soon be joined by another Congregationalist missionary, Luther Rice. Judson looked forward to meeting the now famous William Carey. The new missionary began an intensive study of infant baptism so that he could defend that practice to the Baptist, Carey, but his Biblical study forced him to conclude that the Baptists were right. Luther Rice went through identical circumstances on his trip to India. Both preachers surprised Carey and his associates by presenting themselves for believers' baptism to the Baptist Church in Calcutta, India.

They informed their supporters of their change in doctrine and were immediately cut off from all financial support. The British Government of India refused to allow American missionaries in India, so it was decided that Judson would begin a mission work in Burma and Rice would return to the United States to rally Baptist support for this missions effort.

The Judsons had few converts in the early years of their ministry; however, by 1823, he had translated the New Testament into the Burmese language. Other missionaries joined the Judsons, and there were many converts, baptisms, and a number of churches started. By 1832, Judson restricted himself to translation work and building a seminary for Burmese preachers. Judson and his associates underwent many physical hardships and periods of government persecution.

In the United States, Luther Rice was hard at work organizing the Baptist missions effort. His writing, preaching, and organizational ability influenced many Baptist churches to work together for the cause of missions. This led to the formation of the General Missionary Convention of Baptists. Its first president was an important Baptist leader from South Carolina, Richard Furman. Its purpose was to aid the various Baptist missionaries around the world. The Convention took responsibility for the work of Judson in Burma. They commissioned Isaac McCoy as a missionary to the American Indians, and McCoy experienced tremendous results; however, very few Baptists ever followed him into ministry among the Indians.

Judson led a Karen (a tribe that lived in the hills of Burma) man to Christ who had been a thief and murderer of over 30 men. This man, Ko-Thah-Byu, dedicated himself to learning the Scriptures and brought hundreds of Karen tribesmen into the city to hear new American Baptist missionaries, George and Sara Boardman. This led to missions among the Karen, and soon thousands of Karen converts were ready for baptism. The message spread faster than the missionaries. When the Baptist preachers first arrived at the region of Bassein, they found 5,000 converts ready to present themselves for believers' baptism! Soon, Karen and American missionaries went to the Kachin tribes of northern Burma, resulting in over a quarter of a million Kachins identifying with Christ over the next 90 years.

The people of Lahu, hill people of Burma, China, Laos, and Thailand requested that the Baptists send missionaries to them, and from 1890 until 1936 there were over 2,000 baptisms of the Lahu people every year. The most famous Baptist missionary associated with this movement was William M. Young. Southeast Asia became a strategic area for Christian missionary expansion throughout Asia.

Baptist missions also found heroes among America's black population, even though they were forced to serve in slavery. George Lisle was a slave who was set free by his owner so that he might become a preacher. He was the first ordained Baptist Negro in America, and, in 1778, he started a black Baptist church in Savannah, Georgia. In 1783, he traveled to Jamaica where he started a Baptist church and baptized 500 converts within ten years.

Another former slave was Lott Cary who was allowed to earn the money to buy his freedom after his conversion and his licensing as a preacher. He traveled with the original colonists of Liberia and established the First Baptist Church in Monrovia, the capital city of Liberia.

The Missionary Baptist Convention soon began to support seminaries, Bible colleges, pastoral fellowships, Sunday schools, and engage in fund-raising programs. Great controversy arose among Baptists over the missions movement and the Missionary Convention.

One group opposed the missions movement on the grounds of their view of election. Led by John Taylor and Daniel Parker, they aggressively taught that God had predestined some to Heaven and some to Hell, and they believed that preaching the gospel to the general population was an insult to God. They were often called "hard-shell" or "anti-means" Baptists. This led to bitter disputes among Baptists, and a legal battle was fought over whether the "anti-means" or "means" Baptists had the right to use the name *Regular Baptist*. The Supreme Court finally awarded the right to the name Regular Baptist to the "means" or missions-minded Baptists. The "anti-means" Baptists then took the name *Primitive Baptist*.

Other Baptists supported the idea of missions, but opposed the idea of the General Missionary Convention, fearing that the growing organization, financial structure, and number of projects would make the Convention an authority over local churches. They remained unorganized and supported missions through the program of their local churches and by individually choosing missionaries for their church to support.

The controversy over slavery led the General Missionary Baptist Convention to split along geographic lines forming the Southern Baptist Convention and the Northern Baptist Convention.

Chapter 31

Baptist Controversies

"But thou hast fully known my doctrine, manner of life, purpose, faith, longsuffering, charity, patience, Persecutions, afflictions, which came unto me at Antioch, at Iconium, at Lystra; what persecutions I endured: but out of them all the Lord delivered me. Yea, and all that will live godly in Christ Jesus shall suffer persecution" (2 Timothy 3:10-12).

During the second half of the Nineteenth Century and the first half of the Twentieth Century, Baptists are most remembered for their bitter struggles among themselves. Besides the controversy over "means" versus "anti-means," Baptists battled over:

- slavery,
- education,
- Masonry,
- relationship between baptism and salvation,
- missions,
- liquor, and
- the Second Coming.

In the Twentieth Century, the most crucial struggle was between historic Baptists and those who wished to deny the authority of Scripture and yet still call themselves Baptists.

One of the most dramatic Baptist battles came over Campbellism. Alexander Campbell was born in Ireland and associated there with Presbyterian reformers. He chose to come to the United States so that he might enjoy the religious freedom available to everyone. He became convinced of the error of infant baptism and was baptized by immersion. He began an independent church that soon joined a local Baptist association. Campbell gained a great reputation as a debater.

During this time, Barton W. Stone was dismissed by the Presbyterians because of his doctrine. He taught baptism by immersion of believers only which was contrary to Presbyterian doctrine. He also taught that one had not really believed until he was baptized and that proper baptism was thus necessary for salvation. Campbell and Stone joined forces and began to think of themselves as a Reformation movement among Baptists. Baptists began to debate over the relationship between salvation and baptism, and the doctrine that baptism was essential to salvation became known as *Campbellism.*

A number of Baptist Churches, especially in the South, began to form new groups. The followers of Stone began to consider themselves the "independent Christian" churches, and the followers of Alexander Campbell became known as the Disciples of Christ. The separation between Baptists and the Campbellites was complete. Baptists and Campbellites usually refused to recognize each other's baptism, church membership, and ordination. A later group of Campbellites, dissatisfied with the growing liberalism among the Disciples of Christ, called themselves the Churches of Christ.

Alexander Campbell was originally a strong spokesman against the missions movement but changed his views later. He also spoke against the use of church music and the idea of a call to the ministry.

The question of slavery was a difficult one for Baptists. In England, John Howard, a Baptist pastor, had been a leader for prison reform and a spokesman against slavery in that country. In 1833, English Baptists had led the British West Indies to outlaw slavery, and they called on their American brethren to do the same. As early as 1789, John Leland, the great Baptist preacher associated with our American Constitution, had called for a gradual end to slavery.

Baptists differed greatly in their reaction to slavery issues. Some preached against slavery, but did not consider it
a matter for the local church to deal with, while other
churches accepted slave owners as members but would not
allow them to hold office. Others considered slavery a necessary social evil, while a small group considered slavery
good and ordained of God.

The question haunted relations between preachers.
Could an anti-slavery preacher fellowship with a preacher
who owned slaves? Could he fellowship with a pastor who
did not own slaves but who accepted slave owners in his
church? Tremendous confusion and great differences of
opinion existed among Baptist leaders over this complex issue.

Baptists led the way in abolishing slavery in the northern
states; however, Baptists in the South were among the leaders in fighting to maintain slavery there. The leader of the Illinois Friends to Humanity Association, an anti-slavery
group, was a Baptist preacher who called for all anti-slavery
Baptists to break all fellowship with Baptists who owned
slaves. In Indiana, the leaders of the "Underground Railroad," a system for helping runaway slaves flee to Canada,
were Baptists.

Some of the Baptist missionaries in Burma broke relations with the Missionary Baptist Convention in 1840. The
Convention had sent some missionaries who were slave
owners to the mission field, and they had taken their slaves
with them. Many of the missionaries felt that this greatly
hurt the testimony of the entire Baptist cause in Burma. A
convention of anti-slavery Baptists was held in New York,
and they formed a missionary society to work with those
missionaries who were anti-slavery.

In 1841, the Missionary Baptist Convention issued a
statement of neutrality on the slavery issue, and, in 1844, the
Convention refused to appoint James E. Reeve as a missionary unless he was willing to free the slave he owned. This
caused many southern churches to withdraw from the Con-

vention, and they soon formed their own missionary convention. Most southern Baptist churches, even those who were anti-slavery, felt the need to identify with this Southern Baptist Convention. The outbreak of the Civil War 16 years later did much to make the separation permanent and bitter.

Another prominent battle among Baptists came over the concept of Bible colleges and seminaries. Some Baptists believed that the influence of schools of higher education would cause people to look to the schools instead of the Scripture, and they were afraid that education might destroy the concept of the sole authority of Scripture. The Primitive Baptists as well as the Separate Baptists, identified themselves with this way of thinking. The anti-school Baptists never experienced much growth, and their influence on Baptist affairs in general seemed to diminish with each passing decade. By 1902, there were 36 Baptist universities, 29 Baptist colleges, and seven Baptist seminaries in America.

A sideline debate to the Bible college issue was the battle over the idea of Sunday School. In 1780, Robert Raikes had begun a special school for teaching children on Sunday in London, and a Baptist deacon, William Fox, seized upon the idea and soon Baptist churches all over London had special Sunday morning schools for children. The first recorded Sunday School in the United States was at the Second Baptist Church in Baltimore in 1804. Many churches seemed to feel that this was an excellent way to advance their ministries, although some Baptists, usually those opposed to missions and Bible colleges, felt the schools must be opposed as a "modern" invention. This was a battleground for several decades, but eventually the Sunday School became a regular feature of almost all Baptist churches.

Masonry was another area of controversy among Baptists. Some Baptists considered the Masonic lodges a secret organization of individuals dedicated to the overthrow of the United States. Masons were accused of occult practices and paganism. So many different people throughout the United States felt this way that an anti-Mason political party was formed. Other Baptists believed that the Masons were simply a social organization with no religious significance. The same questions that followed the slavery debate arose again. Should Masons be excluded from church membership, or just church offices, or should they be accepted freely? Could anti-Mason pastors fellowship with neutral pastors? What about pastors who were Masons? The influence of Masons among Baptist Churches gradually diminished, but this controversy still exists in a limited way.

A similar controversy arose over liquor with many Baptists believing that faithful Christians must never use intoxicating drink as a beverage. Some Baptists openly fought this idea as an infringement upon the doctrine of soul liberty. Most of the leadership of the anti-missions group were also pro-alcohol. This was an area of much separation among Baptists, but, by the Twentieth Century, few Baptist preachers openly advocated the use of liquor.

The greatest controversy among Baptists arose in the Twentieth Century. Beginning late in the Nineteenth Century, there arose a group of theologians who carried the name Baptist but denied the authority of Scripture. This was so unheard of that there appears to have been very little awareness of what they were teaching at first. Such Baptist teachers as William N. Clarke, Walter Rauschenbush, Shaller Matthews, and Harry Emerson Fosdick challenged the authority of the Bible and developed a constantly expanding following in Baptist educational circles and in certain large urban churches.

Baptists who belonged to either the Northern or Southern Baptist Convention faced a great dilemma. Should they expel this group from their membership in defense of the doctrine of sole authority of Scripture? Some argued that the doctrine of soul liberty meant that Baptists could not judge one another doctrinally. Since the Conventions took no action, the modernist element within them grew. Many who opposed the modernist element left the conventions and formed new organizations or simply functioned without being a part of any organization. Of course, many Baptists had always done this.

When Ford Porter, a Baptist pastor in Princeton, Indiana, tried to leave the Northern Baptist Convention in protest over modernism, the Convention tried to retain control over his church. This led to a two year legal battle, finally decided by the courts. The court ruled that Baptist churches were, by definition, independent, and that if a majority of the membership wished to withdraw, the Convention could not stop them. This legal decision paved the way for thousands of Baptist churches to withdraw from the two largest Baptist conventions.

The other great controversy among Baptists was over the Second Coming of Christ. Some Baptists were pre-millennialists, believing in the return of Christ to rule and reign upon the earth for 1,000 years, some were post-millennialists, believing that Christ would return after 1,000 years of peace upon the earth, and a smaller number were amillennialist, believing that Christ would return, but that there would be no Millennium. A hundred years of bitter debate separated the three positions. Pre-millennialism eventually became by far the majority position.

The prophetic teaching of one Baptist preacher, William Miller, led many to expect the return of Christ in the 1840's, and when this was proved incorrect, Miller returned to being a normal Baptist teacher. His followers, however, developed into the Seventh Day Adventist cult.

Chapter 32

Baptists and The Rise of Fundamentalism

"*Beloved, when I gave all diligence to write unto you of the common salvation, it was needful for me to write unto you, and exhort you that ye should earnestly contend for the faith which was once delivered unto the saints. For there are certain men crept in unawares, who were before of old ordained to this condemnation, ungodly men, turning the grace of our God into lasciviousness, and denying the only Lord God, and our Lord Jesus Christ*" (Jude 3-4).

The earliest challenges of modernism to the Baptist movement had little success; however, the issue of modernism arose over and over again in Baptist colleges. Soon, three distinct movements developed.

- Those who clearly held to the basic historic doctrines of the Christian faith and who insisted that these truths be a basis for fellowship were called Fundamentalists.

The doctrines that they considered "fundamental" were the inerrancy of Scripture, the deity of Christ, the Trinity, the virgin birth, the atonement, Christ's bodily resurrection, and the Second Coming. Many early Baptist Fundamentalists also emphasized pre-millennialism.

Baptist Fundamentalists all believed that the modernists had the right to teach as they pleased (religious liberty), but they rejected their right to do so in Baptist schools. They believed that Baptist conventions and other organizations should adopt clear doctrinal statements covering the fundamentals of the Christian faith and the Baptist distinctives and expel modernists.

- The second group was the modernists themselves.

The modernists plainly felt that Scripture was not authoritative and, consequently, all ideas and principles were relative. They continually claimed that the Baptist doctrines of soul liberty and the priesthood of all believers gave them the right to teach anything they pleased and still be considered good Baptists.

- A third group called themselves "moderates."

They believed in the basic fundamentals, but they were opposed to the idea of a doctrinal statement being used as a basis for fellowship. They believed that where truth and error co-existed, truth would always triumph. They also felt that maintaining political unity within their organizations was more important than maintaining doctrinal purity.

Battle lines were drawn. From 1910 to 1915, a series of books were written to make clear the fundamentals. This battle was also being fought among the Methodists, Presbyterians, Lutherans, and Episcopalians, as well as the Baptists. Baptist Fundamentalists were led by prominent pastors of large churches like William Bell Riley, I. M. Haldeman, John R. Straton, and T. T. Shields. Within the Northern Baptist Convention, Southern Baptist Convention, National Baptist Convention, and Canadian Baptist Convention, the battle raged. Battles took place for control of missionary organizations, colleges, and seminaries.

The great question faced by the Fundamentalists was how long they should struggle for establishment of a strong doctrinal position before giving up and withdrawing from their respective conventions. This question never received a final answer.

The first church to leave a convention in protest of modernism appears to be the Wealthy Street Baptist Church of Grand Rapids, Michigan in 1909. This church left the Northern Baptist Convention because there was no clear doctrinal position for their colleges. The question is still being debated, and 90 years later there are still churches leaving their respective denominations in protest over the influence of modernism.

The great battles for control did not seem to go the way of the Fundamentalists. The Southern Baptist Convention did adopt a clear doctrinal statement in 1925, but it was also made clear that no provisions for enforcement would be put into practice. This did create a more conservative atmosphere within the Southern Baptist Convention than the other large conventions. It did not end the battle over modernism, however, for many modernists clearly stayed active within the Southern Baptist Convention. The other conventions did not adopt any creed, and individual churches continue to leave conventions to this day.

Fundamentalists formed the Baptist Bible Union under the leadership of T. T. Shields, and its expressed purpose was to battle modernism on all fronts. The Union sponsored the beginning of a new seminary and provided a forum for fundamental Baptists. For several years, the Baptist Bible Union made it possible for fundamental Baptists from several different conventions to work together against modernism.

Finally, the Northern Baptist Convention went to court to stop Dr. Ford Porter's church, the First Baptist Church of Princeton, Indiana, from leaving the Convention in protest over modernism. When this strategy failed, and the rights of the church were upheld by the court, the stage was set for massive withdrawals from the major conventions.

In 1933, over 50 churches left the Northern Baptist Convention and formed the General Association of Regular Baptist Churches (commonly known as the GARBC). Robert Ketcham became a strong leader within the GARBC. His influence led the GARBC to two very important decisions. First, the new organization would not be in the form of a convention, but in the form of a much looser-knit fellowship. This would make it more difficult for any central or state organization to interfere with the independence of member churches.

Secondly, no church would be allowed to maintain membership in both the Northern Baptist Convention and the GARBC. This was done to maintain a clear philosophy of separation in the new fellowship. Several colleges were approved, and several mission agencies formed. The GARBC continued to grow as each year more churches left the conventions.

It is impossible to discuss the rise of Baptist Fundamentalism without discussing J. Frank Norris. Norris was a tremendous preacher, brilliant organizer, and a very colorful spokesman against modernism. He was an outstanding church builder, and his church-building methods influenced a generation of preachers. He thrived on controversy, and he was engaged in notable controversies with Roman Catholicism, the liquor traffic, evolutionists, both the moderate and the modernist crowd in the Southern Baptist Convention, and with several other Fundamentalist leaders. He was charged with both arson and murder in the courts, but he was acquitted of all charges.

Norris began a very strong and open battle with the Southern Baptist Convention in general, and the state convention in Texas in particular. Such prominent Southern Baptist church-builders as George W. Truett and L. R. Scarborough answered the attacks by Norris. Eventually, Norris was expelled from the national and state conventions. He devoted the rest of his life to battling the Convention and its modernistic influences. Whenever the Southern Baptists held their national convention, Norris rented a large auditorium and held meetings in the same city. He preached against the Convention, and he usually drew larger crowds than the Convention did!

Norris applied for admission for his church to the GARBC and was refused, so he formed the World Baptist Fellowship. Soon, many churches left the Southern Baptist Convention to join this new fundamental Baptist fellowship. In 1934, Norris was pastor of the church with the largest attendance of any in the United States. This was the First Baptist Church of Fort Worth, Texas. He also accepted the pastorate of the Temple Baptist Church in Detroit, Michigan, even though they were 1,300 miles apart! Within three years, Temple Baptist was the second largest church in the country. This was an absolutely unique accomplishment for any church-builder. In addition to pastoring the two largest churches in the nation, Norris then started the Bible Baptist Seminary at his church in Fort Worth.

Norris was involved in many battles with his fellow fundamental Baptists. He was responsible for very serious attacks on John R. Rice, a leader among independent Baptists, Robert Ketcham, leader of the GARBC, and G. Beauchamp Vick, who had succeeded Dr. Norris at Temple Baptist in Detroit. (Vick was also one of the founders of the Baptist Bible Fellowship.) All three men stated that their controversies with Norris were the greatest spiritual battles they ever faced.

Finally, in 1950, many of the leaders of the World Baptist Fellowship broke with Norris and formed the Baptist Bible Fellowship. This organization became strongly identified with aggressive church-building. It runs or approves several colleges and maintains its own missions board. The Baptist Bible Fellowship quickly became the largest organization of fundamental Baptists in the world.

Another group of Baptists left the Northern Baptist Convention and called themselves the Conservative Baptists. The lines now seemed to be drawn. There were five general classifications of Baptists:

- those smaller groups which had never belonged to the large conventions (e.g., Regular, Primitive, Separate, United Baptists, etc.);
- the large conventions (with the role of modernists firmly established);
- the fundamentalist Baptist fellowships (e.g., GARBC, WBF, BBF, Conservative Baptists);

- a growing number of independent, non-aligned Baptists; and,
- those Baptists known as "Landmarkers."

The movement called Landmarkism actually began in the mid-1800's. Led by James R. Graves and Jim Pendelton, these Baptists took a strong exclusivist view. They went further than the common Baptist view that Baptists represented the best, most consistent expression of New Testament Christianity. They believed that Baptists were the only New Testament Christians and would not fellowship with any non-Baptists. Many would not fellowship with any who were not Landmarkers, and many carried that thought further and believed that Baptists have a special place in Heaven. This movement experienced a great amount of growth as Baptists left their respective conventions and associated with Landmarkism. Certainly there was no question of modernism among the Landmarkers.

One new aspect of the fundamentalist-modernist debate soon emerged that is called new-evangelicalism. New-evangelicalism is a philosophy similar to that of the moderates in the great disputes within the conventions. New-evangelicals maintain a commitment to the concept of personal salvation. They maintain at least some concept of loyalty to the idea of an inspired Bible; however, they advocate trying to find a common ground for fellowship with various religious philosophies and doctrines. This controversy has had a great impact on Baptists.

The leading spokesman for the new-evangelical position is a Baptist — the well known evangelist, Billy Graham. Graham, easily the most famous preacher in the United States, openly held city-wide crusades sponsored by modernists as well as doctrinal conservatives. It was not unusual to see modernists, Roman Catholics, Seventh Day Adventists, charismatics, and evangelicals from various groups united in a Billy Graham Crusade.

This philosophy created a number of questions for Baptists. Should a Baptist participate in such a program? If he refuses, as the fundamental Baptists do, can he fellowship with those Baptists who do choose to participate? Such questions led to a serious split within the Conservative Baptist movement.

Evangelist John R. Rice spoke out against fellowship with new-evangelical crusades but left the door open for fellowship with Bible believers who did fellowship in such programs. He published and edited a widely distributed paper, *The Sword of the Lord*. This paper had a tremendous amount of influence in the fundamental Baptist movement. Many Baptist Fundamentalists have drawn stricter lines of separation than Dr. Rice did.

Modernism overwhelmed the Baptist movement in England, most European countries, and Canada. It did not have such total victory in the United States. Modernism did, however, draw many who were called Baptists away from the historic Baptist faith.

The National Baptist Convention, Canadian Baptist Convention, and the Northern Baptist Convention came to be dominated by modernism. The battle is still being fought within the Southern Baptist Convention. The annual meeting of the Southern Baptist Convention each year features new battles between modernists, moderates, and doctrinally conservative Southern Baptists. The final lesson of that story has not yet been written.

(It should certainly be noted that many have used the Scriptural term "Landmark" while not holding to all the positions of Landmarkism.)

Chapter 33

Other Baptist Developments

"We are troubled on every side, yet not distressed; we are perplexed, but not in despair; Persecuted, but not forsaken; cast down, but not destroyed; Always bearing about in the body the dying of the Lord Jesus, that the life also of Jesus might be made manifest in our body" (2 Corinthians 4:8-10).

The story of black Baptist churches in the United States deserves special notice. From the very beginning, the reaction of Baptist churches to slavery and slaves had been controversial. The church that Roger Williams pastored had Negro slaves in its membership. Some churches admitted slaves as members just like any free person, while other churches admitted slaves but held separate services for them. Other white churches started separate churches for slaves. Many large plantations had their own churches. Unfortunately, many churches ignored Negroes altogether.

Baptists seemed to have special success with the Negro population. Perhaps the Baptist concepts of individual soul liberty and religious freedom had a special appeal to those who were daily reminded of what it was like not to be free. Certainly the Baptists (along with the Methodists) put more time and money into Negro ministries than other groups. The Baptist movement continued to grow among Negroes in America until Turner's Revolt.

Nat Turner was a black Baptist preacher who led a group of black slaves into armed revolt. He correctly preached that the Baptist distinctives logically demanded freedom for all. He incorrectly thought that he could lead all blacks into an organized revolt and that they would be joined by sympathetic whites from the northern states and Europe. He also foolishly assumed that God and man would overlook wanton acts of violence committed in the name of freedom. His revolt, after causing the deaths of over 30 whites, was soon violently and totally crushed. Even though most black Baptists rejected Turner's ideas, there was a great reaction against black Baptist churches throughout the South.

As had been the case with the Kingdom of Munster in Sixteenth Century Germany, and the Fifth Monarchy rebellion in Seventeenth Century England, the excesses of a handful were used as an excuse to persecute innocent Baptists. Black Baptist churches throughout the South were closed — some temporarily and some permanently. Many slaves were forbidden by plantation owners to attend church, especially Baptist churches.

Many blacks ran to the North looking for the freedom that would be theirs if they could reach Canada. A large number of the runaways were Baptists. Many northerners helped them travel to Canada through a system called the "Underground Railroad." In Indiana, the participants in the Underground Railroad were almost entirely Baptists who felt an obligation to their black Baptist brothers and sisters in Christ. This led to a number of black Baptist churches in Canada.

After the Civil War, a number of black Baptist associations, conventions, and missionary organizations were formed. By 1935, these were almost all united in the National Baptist Convention. In 1915, this organization split into two conventions, each claiming to be the true National Baptist Convention. This still causes much confusion today. A third major black convention was formed later by blacks who were anxious for a greater emphasis on social reform. Modernism and the concept of the social gospel have gained great inroads within the black Baptist conventions. The two most prominent black Baptist leaders of recent years have been Martin Luther King, Jr. and Jesse Jackson.

Neither emphasized the fundamental Christian faith. Their primary focus has been on political and social reform. King was assassinated in 1968, and Jackson is best known for his prominence in the Democrat Party. He was a candidate for President of the United States during the primaries of 1988.

While modernism has made great progress in the organizations of all the black Baptist conventions, many individual black Baptist Christians and many black Baptist churches still maintain their respect for the fundamentals of the Christian faith and the historic Baptist distinctives.

Because we rarely hear of Baptist martyrs anymore in our western civilization, it is easy for us to forget that many Baptists are still paying for their faith with their own blood. Probably more Baptists have been killed during the Twentieth Century than any other time.

Miss Lottie Moon was a Southern Baptist missionary in China for 40 years and, during the great famine in China in 1911-1912, she refused to eat while many Chinese around her were starving. She eventually starved to death! Every year the Southern Baptist Convention remembers her as they take up their annual foreign missions offering in her name.

There were many Christians in China, and a number of Baptist churches had formed their own associations and built their own university. During the Boxer Rebellion (Chinese opposing any foreigners being in China), many missionaries were killed. Baptist churches were burned and a number of Chinese Baptists were beaten and robbed by the Boxers. This set back the entire Christian cause in China.

After the Boxer Rebellion ended, a Communist uprising broke out in China. The Communists assassinated Christian pastors and burned their church buildings. Again, a number of Baptist churches were affected. After the Japanese invaded China, the Chinese Communists and the government declared an uneasy truce.

Missionaries were forced to leave the areas of China occupied by the Japanese and after the United States entered the war, American missionaries were seized by the Japanese and were imprisoned. Chinese Baptists refused to acknowledge the Japanese government, and many were killed. Dr. Herman Liu, president of the Baptist University, was executed in his front yard. Baptist churches in occupied areas were closed. This was the third wave of persecution in less than 30 years; however, the worst was yet to come.

After the war, the Communist rebellion began again, and an American Baptist missionary, John Birch, was killed by the Communists. After the Communists took control of China, most missionaries were expelled, and the others disappeared never to be heard from again. Baptist missionary doctor, Bill Wallace, died while in a Communist prison, but the Red Chinese claimed he committed suicide.

Many Baptist churches were closed in China, and many Christians were executed. (Most estimates run into the millions!) Some churches were allowed to remain open so that a show of religious liberty could be maintained. The Baptist University was permitted to remain open, but its president, Henry Liu (brother of Herman Liu), was arrested again. He died in a Communist prison in 1960. Despite massive persecutions and executions, the evangelical churches in China still exist. Reports constantly come out of China concerning independent churches, and many Chinese Baptists still meet in secret in the mountains and wilderness areas along the southern Chinese coast.

Today, China claims to have reinstituted religious freedom, but it is very limited. Christians are permitted to openly worship in some regions of China (usually those which receive the most tourists). In other regions, the same past persecution seems to exist. Most dedicated Christians attend illegal house churches in secret.

The large number of Baptists in Burma, the country of Adoniram Judson, was reduced during a revolution against the Burmese government. The hill tribes, where most of the Baptists were, tried to establish an independent state, but were defeated. Today, Burma is closed to American missionaries, but there are still over 300,000 reported Baptists meeting in native churches in Burma.

Throughout Asia, most Baptist churches have come from recent missionary activity. In South Korea and some areas of the Philippines, Baptists have been particularly successful.

It is said that the largest Baptist churches in the world are in South Korea. Dr. Viggo Olsen, a Baptist medical missionary, has become well known for his very successful medical mission in Bangladesh.

In the Middle East, most countries are closed to missionaries and there is little Baptist influence. Baptist missionaries in Israel are severely limited, especially those to the Arabs. Baptist witness is maintained in Lebanon and Jordan, and King Hussein of Jordan, a Moslem leader, has consistently educated his children in Baptist schools.

In Africa, most Baptist churches are related to the missionary activities of British and American Baptists over the last hundred years. Many African countries are now closed to missionaries. African Baptists are harassed in some nations by Moslem governments and in others by Communist governments. Many missionaries rejoiced when N'Garta Tombalbaye became the first President of Chad. He was a professing member of a Baptist church and had taught in a Baptist school run by missionaries. However, he assumed dictatorial powers and tried to enforce Yondo, a primitive tribal religion, as the new state church. He immediately began to persecute Baptists who refused to cooperate and finally forced all Baptist missionaries out of the country. Many native believers were killed, some by horrible tortures. He was finally assassinated, and the missionaries were permitted to return. Throughout the last hundred years, many Christians have been killed during regional persecutions such as this one in Chad.

Some African countries have remained open to missions without any persecution. Liberia, Nigeria, Sierre Leone, and Kenya all have a number of well-established Baptist works. In Angola, there were two well-established rebellions against the Communist government, one headed by a Baptist, Holden Roberto. The Communist government of Angola executed a number of Baptist and Plymouth Brethren pastors for their faith. In modern Malawi, native Baptists led a revolution which overthrew the European government and established a black government. In nearby Zimbabwe (old Rhodesia), the revolution came under Communist control, and Baptists were often targets for Communist guerrillas. One American Baptist missionary was killed.

In South Africa, Baptists have been very divided with some supporting the former white government and others pushing for moderate reform government. Some Baptist pastors have been arrested for integrating churches. A growing number of Communist revolutionaries threaten Christians in that country. Religious freedom was put in a precarious state with the election of Nelson Mandela as President of South Africa.

In Cuba, Baptists were very successful until the Communist revolution under Castro. By 1965, all Baptist pastors in Cuba had been arrested, and most American Baptist missionaries were expelled from the country. David Fite and Herbert Caudill were imprisoned, and four years later they were released as a result of international pressure upon the government of Castro. Some Baptist pastors have been released, and some church activities are allowed.

In Haiti, there are many Baptist works. One of the leaders in the overthrow of Papa Doc Duvalier was a Baptist preacher who had graduated from a fundamental Bible college in America. Very recent turmoil in Haiti has left the situation for Baptist missionaries in jeopardy. Baptists are also very active in the Dominican Republic where Baptist missionaries, Paul and Nancy Potter, were killed by leftist terrorists in 1971.

The first Baptist missionaries went to Mexico in the 1860's, and one of them, John Westrup, was murdered by fanatic Catholics. Many regions of Mexico have been open to Baptists, and numerous Baptist missionaries work there. Most Central American countries are open to missionaries, and there are a number of Baptist missionaries in that area. In Marxist Nicaragua, most missionaries were banished, and many pastors were harassed. Many evangelicals identified with the *Contra* revolution to regain freedom in that country.

Baptist churches in South America are also related to missionary activity of the last century. Baptists have often been harassed by Roman Catholic governments, but they usually are allowed to operate.

Of course, the greatest source of Baptist martyrs in the Twentieth Century has been Soviet Russia. For four years after the Soviet revolution, Lenin promoted religious freedom. Then he began a persecution that led to literally millions of executions for religious reasons over the following 30 years. One prominent Baptist evangelist, Cornelius Martens, was banished from the country after he received a great amount of publicity. After World War II, the Soviets executed many Baptists throughout Eastern Europe. A Baptist pastor, Georgi Vins, expelled from Russia, became an international spokesman for persecuted Baptists in Russia.

Since the overthrow of Communism in the former Soviet Union and many Eastern bloc countries, many Baptists have conducted missionary trips leading multiplied thousands to Christ and distributing millions of Bibles. Many fundamental Baptists are going to Eastern European countries as full-time missionaries. The prayer among all concerned about missions is that the door will stay open in these formerly Communist countries.

Chapter 34

Baptist Expansion: Church Builders and Christian Education

"But none of these things move me, neither count I my life dear unto myself, so that I might finish my course with joy, and the ministry, which I have received of the Lord Jesus, to testify the gospel of the grace of God" (Acts 20:24).

❖ ❖ ❖

Fundamental Baptists have become famous over the last 30 years for their ability to build large churches. Because of this influence, a large church is no longer thought of as running several hundred in attendance. A large church today is one that runs several thousand. Several factors have influenced this burst of building large churches.

The example of Charles Haddon Spurgeon in England undoubtedly influenced many Baptists in America. The large numbers that Spurgeon drew changed the scope of his ministry, and he became a national spokesman for the cause of Christ. Politicians became concerned about his opinion, and various causes sought his recognition and support. The public noticed everything his church did. Several thousand people concentrated in one church seemed to have a greater impact than the same number spread over a number of churches. His church was also large enough to support a college.

In the United States, two radically different Southern Baptists built large churches in Texas. Both emphasized aggressive evangelism. George W. Truett, pastor of First Baptist Church of Dallas, Texas, was an eloquent leader of the Southern Baptist Convention and a great church-builder. He was known for being congenial and "building bridges" to many different groups in the community. He was succeeded by W. A. Criswell who has continued to build the church to one of the largest in the nation and who has continued to be a leader in the Southern Baptist Convention.

We have already studied J. Frank Norris who was a master of using controversy to build church attendance. Once, during one of his frequent battles with the local liquor industry, one of his chief opponents was killed in an accident caused by the influence of liquor. His brains were literally splattered on a public sidewalk, and someone scraped up some of the brain tissue and put it in a jar of formaldehyde. It was given to Norris who displayed the jar on his pulpit, advertised it, and announced he would be preaching on the results of using alcohol. He drew a tremendous crowd.

Norris used other methods besides controversy to stir church growth. He made popular the ideas of door-to-door visitation, building attendance through Sunday School visitation, preparing his own Sunday School literature, transportation ministry, and an aggressive youth ministry. His influence is still felt in churches throughout the country. Norris changed an entire generation of preachers' attitudes about church growth.

A third major influence was that of *The Sword of the Lord*. Editor and publisher, John R. Rice, used his paper to constantly promote the idea of revival, soul-winning, and church growth. Dr. Rice and Dr. Bob Jones, Sr. traveled the country promoting soul-winning in conferences for pastors. Rice called attention to churches that were growing, and he gave an opportunity for successful pastors to share their ideas and methods with a large audience in *Sword* conferences.

Dr. Curtis Hutson followed Dr. Rice as editor of *The Sword of the Lord* and continued the emphasis on revival and soul-winning until his death in 1995.

After Dr. Jones was no longer able to travel with him, Dr. Rice was usually joined by Dr. Jack Hyles, pastor of First Baptist Church in Hammond, Indiana. His church is generally considered to be the largest Baptist church in the world, averaging over 20,000 in Sunday School! Without a doubt, Dr. Hyles has been a fourth major influence in the large church movement. After building a very large church in Garland (near Dallas), Texas (where he had been dropped from the Southern Baptist Convention for his opposition to modernism within the Convention), he took the pastorate of the First Baptist Church in Hammond. His ministry in Hammond drastically influenced the concept of church-building in America. He led First Baptist Church in Hammond into having the largest average weekly attendance in the United States of all denominations! His strong teaching on personal soul-winning, door-to-door evangelism, Sunday School visitation, bus ministry, and specialized church programs (deaf ministry, Hispanic ministry, etc.) created an atmosphere for tremendous growth. His organizational ability has held a many faceted ministry together with incredible cohesion. More than that, many people have felt that the Lord especially used Dr. Hyles to motivate them to soul-winning and church-building.

Dr. Hyles' ideas have been spread through *The Sword of the Lord* and similar conferences, his many books, his annual Pastors' School (attended by thousands), and a college sponsored by his church, Hyles-Anderson College.

The United States has seen many other large churches built by Baptists. In 1969, the nine churches in the U. S. with the largest weekly attendance were Baptist (eight of them independent, one Southern Baptist). In 1979, 13 of the 20 largest churches were Baptist.

Another noted church-builder has been Dr. Lee Roberson who pastored the Highland Park Baptist Church in Chattanooga, Tennessee, for over 40 years, beginning in 1942 when the Sunday School averaged 470. In 1979, the church averaged 11,000 in Sunday School! Dr. Roberson's ideas about church growth have also been spread through his many speaking engagements and his Baptist college, Tennessee Temple University.

Dr. John Rawlings and the Landmark Baptist Temple in Cincinnati, Ohio, also influenced the church growth movement. Dr. Rawlings has been a leader of the Baptist Bible Fellowship from its very beginning. He led in the building of a church of several thousand in Cincinnati.

The Baptist Bible Fellowship has been associated with a number of pastors who have built large churches. Their first college, Baptist Bible College of Springfield, Missouri, has been known for training church-builders. Besides Dr. Rawlings, other Baptist Bible Fellowship pastors known for building large churches have included:

- Dr. G. B. Vick, pastor of Temple Baptist in Detroit, Michigan;
- Dr. Charles Billington, pastor of Akron Baptist Temple, Akron, Ohio;
- Dr. Harold Henniger, pastor of Canton Baptist Temple, Canton, Ohio, and
- Dr. Jerry Falwell, pastor of Thomas Road Baptist Church in Lynchburg, Virginia.

Dr. G. B. Vick was president of Baptist Bible College for many years and was credited with influencing the college's emphasis on church growth.

Another important leader of the Baptist Bible Fellowship was Dr. Noel Smith who served as editor of the *Baptist Bible Tribune* until his death.

Dr. Jerry Falwell has made a tremendous impact on the American public. When the media wants to get a fundamental Baptist reaction on any issue, they usually turn to Dr. Falwell for comment. Besides being known as a church builder, Dr. Falwell has a national television ministry, and, as a result, has become as well-known as any pastor in the nation. He has also built a large, accredited university, Liberty University, connected with his church. He influenced many Baptists and other fundamentalists to political involvement through his political organization, Moral Majority (now called Liberty Foundation). Dr. Falwell has had many critics from both within and without the fundamental Baptist movement, but no one can deny his impact on the nation as a whole.

With the rise of the large churches came an incredible growth in the Christian day school movement. Widespread dissatisfaction with the level of education and the lack of discipline in most public schools led many fundamental Baptists to "rethink" education. Thousands of Baptist churches started their own schools, and while many of them were small and facilities and equipment were limited, these schools were usually superior to the public schools! In 1989, Landmark Baptist Church in Haines City, Florida, pastored by Dr. Mickey P. Carter, became the first Baptist church to offer a complete Christian day school and homeschool curriculum. Landmark's Freedom Baptist Curriculum is unique as a Baptist curriculum and is growing in influence across America and throughout the world.

Christian education became a major issue for fundamental Baptists, and the first major source of conflict with the state in decades. Federal and local governments claimed authority over education that many Baptists felt belonged only to parents, so conflicts occurred in many states leading to important legal battles. Separation of church and state and religious freedom were often upheld by the courts, yet the issues and harassment never seemed to disappear. Many Baptist church and school ministries were defended by a Baptist preacher/attorney named David Gibbs, Jr. Gibbs's Christian Law Association became "legal missionaries" for numerous ministries. The final lesson to this issue has yet to be written.

A tremendous growth in Christian higher education also occurred during this time. Many Bible colleges grew, and a large number of Baptist colleges and universities have been started.

Great advances have also been made in the realm of the

media. Among the many religious leaders to make use of television, besides Dr. Falwell, have been Southern Baptist evangelist John Ankerberg, Southern Baptist pastor Charles Stanley, and independent Baptist Jack Van Impe. Local television broadcasts are becoming more and more common for Baptist Churches. Local and national radio ministries have been common for Baptists for many years. Oliver B. Greene and Lester Roloff are two fundamental Baptists who have had widely received radio broadcasts.

Fundamental Baptists have also developed a number of missions agencies. The Baptist Bible Fellowship, Conservative Baptists, and World Baptist Fellowship maintain their own missionary societies, while other Baptist mission boards include:

- Association of Baptists for World Evangelism,
- Baptist International Missions,
- Baptist Mid-Missions,
- Baptist World Mission,
- Evangelical Baptist Mission, and
- Maranatha Baptist Mission.

An organization devoted to spreading the Scriptures throughout the world, operating out of Baptist churches, is Bearing Precious Seed.

Chapter 35

Baptist Organizations

"And what agreement hath the temple of God with idols? for ye are the temple of the living God; as God hath said, I will dwell in them, and walk in them; and I will be their God, and they shall be my people. Wherefore come out from among them, and be ye separate, saith the Lord, and touch not the unclean thing; and I will receive you, And will be a Father unto you, and ye shall be my sons and daughters, saith the Lord Almighty" (2 Corinthians 6:17-18).

❖❖❖

BAPTIST ORGANIZATIONS IN AMERICA

Southern Baptist Convention

The largest Baptist group in the United States organized on the basis of state conventions is the Southern Baptist Convention. They maintain a large missionary program called the Cooperative Program (descended from the Missionary Baptist Convention). Many colleges, seminaries, camps, and other ministries are operated by the state conventions. This group is constantly engaged in an internal battle about the nature of Scripture. There are more than 13 million Southern Baptists in America.

National Baptist Convention, U.S.A.

This is the second largest Baptist group in the United States, and is composed primarily of black Baptists. Marked by an internal struggle over modernism, this group is very social gospel-oriented. It has over five million members in the United States.

National Baptist Convention of America

This group also represents black Baptists and has similar internal conflicts to the NBC, USA. Its approach to the ministry is also similar to the NBC. It is very active in social programs and has over two and a half million members.

Baptist Bible Fellowship

This is a loose-knit fellowship of Baptist pastors and the largest Baptist group without any modernist element. They have their own mission board and a list of approved colleges located from coast to coast. State fellowships often maintain their own camps and other projects. The group's membership is estimated at over two million. This group split from the World Baptist Fellowship.

American Baptist Convention

This group was formerly called the Northern Baptist Convention and is organized along the lines of state conventions. It is active in most states, and it approves many colleges, seminaries, and mission projects that are controlled by state conventions. Modernism has become dominant in this group. It has about one and a half million members.

American Baptist Association

This group is very strong in the South, especially in Arkansas and Texas. Most of the ABA preachers are Landmarkers, and its membership is estimated at over 700,000. They operate a number of Bible institutes and colleges.

World Baptist Fellowship

This group was founded by J. Frank Norris as a split from the Southern Baptist Convention. It is solidly Fundamentalist with over 700,000 members. They operate their own college in Texas.

National Primitive Baptist Convention

This group is made up of black Baptists who originally

adopted Primitive Baptist positions during the great "means" versus "anti-means" debate. Today, it faces similar circumstances as other black Baptist groups except that it does not maintain schools. It has over 700,000 members.

Progressive National Baptist Convention

This is another black Baptist convention. It was recently formed with the strongest emphasis on the social gospel and modernism. It has over 500,000 members.

General Association of Regular Baptist Churches

This is a doctrinally conservative group of independent Baptist churches that was formed when Fundamentalists left the Northern Baptist Convention in protest over modernism. It is formed along state organizational lines with each state group controlling its own camps and other projects. It maintains an approved list of mission boards and colleges. It has over 300,000 members. Most of them are located in the North.

Conservative Baptist Association of America

This is another group of doctrinally conservative Baptists who left the Northern Baptist Convention in protest over modernism. It began with a separate missions society and is often thought of as presenting a middle-of-the-road approach between modernist Baptists and strong Fundamentalists. It is estimated that they have over 300,000 members.

Baptist Missionary Association

The word "missionary" originally identified their support of the "means" side during the "means" versus "anti-means" controversy. This group was formed during 1950 as a split off the American Baptist Association. It has over 200,000 members, and they take the position called Landmarkism.

Freewill Baptists

This group is Arminian, and they trace their movement back to Randall in the Nineteenth Century. Many Freewill Baptists merged with the Northern Baptists in the early Twentieth Century, but this group maintained a clear Fundamentalist, separatist position. It maintains a college in Tennessee, and it has over 200,000 members.

Baptist General Conference of America

This group is also called Swedish Baptist because their church services were originally in the Swedish language. It was formed as a great many Swedes came to the United States during the second half of the Nineteenth Century. They merged with the Northern Baptist Convention but broke away during the Twentieth Century in protest over modernism among the Northern Baptists. They have over 110,000 members.

General Baptists

This group is Arminian, and they trace their association back to the General Baptists of England. It maintains a college in Oakland City, Indiana, and has about 90,000 members.

Primitive Baptists

This is a group of Calvinist, anti-missionary Baptists found mostly in the South and Midwest. They are anti-Bible college and have over 75,000 members.

United Baptists

This group was formed by the merger of some Regular and Separate Baptists in the Virginia colony. Most of these are in the South and Midwest with over 60,000 members.

Regular Baptists

This group traces its associations to the earliest English colonies and has over 20,000 members.

Separate Baptists

This is another group of Arminian Baptists who trace their heritage to the Great Awakening in Virginia. It is anti-Bible college and has over 10,000 members.

Seventh Day Baptists

This group holds worship services on Saturday and traces its heritage to the early colonies. It has over 5,000 members.

Southwide Baptist Fellowship

This organization of Fundamentalist Baptists meets yearly for fellowship and edification. They do not have an official school or mission board, and it is possible to belong to other Baptist fellowships concurrently. It puts a strong emphasis on church building and evangelism.

Fundamental Baptist Fellowship

This group of Baptists takes a very strong position on separation. It is known for labeling a segment of the Baptist movement as pseudo-fundamentalist.

Independent Baptist Fellowship International

Many former World Baptist Fellowship preachers split to form the IBFI in the 1980's. They are fundamental in doctrine and operate a Bible institute (named for J. Frank Norris) and missions board in Ft. Worth, Texas. They emphasize church-building, missions, and soul-winning.

INTERNATIONAL BAPTIST ORGANIZATIONS

Baptist World Alliance

This group was designed to provide a forum for Baptists worldwide to maintain a united testimony and to carry out joint projects. Different Baptist groups from 115 nations and representing 31 million Baptists are members. Most fundamentalists avoid this group because of its toleration of modernism.

European Baptist Federation

This group was organized in 1949 to provide a common testimony for European Baptists. It represents over 800,000 Baptists and maintains a missionary society. However, it is heavily influenced by modernists.

BAPTIST ORGANIZATIONS IN OTHER NATIONS

Baptist Bible Union of Great Britain

This group consists of over 2,000 churches and maintains colleges and a missionary society. It is solidly modernistic and has over 175,000 members.

Baptist Federation of Canada

This group has over 1,000 churches, maintains schools, social programs, and a missionary society. It is heavily modernistic. It has over 150,000 members.

Many countries of the world have their own Baptist Conventions (e.g., the Argentina Baptist Convention, the Baptist Union of South Africa, etc.). Some of these affiliate with the Southern Baptist Convention in the United States. Most churches started by Fundamentalist Baptist missionaries do not join national conventions. This is because most (if not all) national conventions contain modernists, and God warns us to "come out from among them and be ye separate" (II Corinthians 6:17).

Chapter 36

Baptist Heroes Inspire us to the Future

"And when he had opened the fifth seal, I saw under the altar the souls of them that were slain for the word of God, and for the testimony which they held: And they cried with a loud voice, saying, How long, O Lord, holy and true, dost thou not judge and avenge our blood on them that dwell on the earth?" (Revelation 6:9-10).

George Mueller is remembered as a great hero of the Christian faith. His work of building orphanages in England and his life of faith were a sterling testimony for Christ. After he had begun his famous ministry in Bristol, England, he became convinced of the truth of believers' baptism; however, he knew that most of his financial support came from those who accepted infant baptism. He knew that presenting himself for believers' baptism would be a humbling experience for one who was already a well-known preacher. He also knew his financial support would suffer. But, he was convinced that this was Scriptural, so he presented himself for baptism. His ministry did suffer for a while, but it was his testimony that he knew he had been obedient to the Lord.

Dr. Bob Jones, Sr. was a well-known evangelist, ordained by the Methodist Church. He preached meetings with the support of a wide variety of Fundamentalist churches. He was well known as an advocate of believers' baptism, but he was criticized for not surrendering his Methodist ordination. (The Methodists held to a position of infant baptism.) Jones continued to preach this truth as a Methodist and found himself receiving the support of many Baptists. He eventually founded Bob Jones University, an interdenominational school where many Baptists were educated.

B. H. Carroll fought in the Confederate Army during the Civil War until he was wounded. Reacting to a dare in 1865, he attended a camp meeting, was converted and baptized in a Baptist church. He became famous as a pastor and as a Baptist theologian and did more to encourage fundamental Baptist doctrine among Southern Baptists than any other man.

When John Birch was a young college student at Mercer University, he was appalled by the modernism there. He formed a fellowship of young Baptist students to protest the unbelief they found in this Baptist college. However, the college refused to permit the fellowship to meet. Statements by Birch led to an investigation of modernism at Mercer, and much controversy followed. Birch identified with J. Frank Norris and received training at Baptist Bible Seminary for the mission field.

Birch went to China as a missionary and was working in an area that was taken over by the Japanese in their invasion of China during World War II. Birch eventually had to flee to Free China where he volunteered to work with the Chinese Army rescuing downed pilots. He soon was rescuing American pilots who had to bail out over China after bombing Japan. He is the one who found the famous Jimmy Doolittle and his crew after their famous bombing raid on Tokyo. Birch continued with missionary preaching while working for the Chinese and then the American military. One week after the war ended, Birch was killed by Chinese Communists. The true story of his death was hidden by our government for five years. In the late 1950's, a new anti-Communist organization took Birch's name as a symbol of the fight against Communism. They call themselves the John Birch Society.

R. A. Torrey was well known as a great soul-winning evangelist, pastor, and Christian educator. He was from a Presbyterian background, had been sprinkled as an infant, and ordained as a Congregationalist. He was already a nationally famous preacher when his own study of Scripture convinced him of believers' baptism. He and his wife humbled themselves, admitting that they had never been properly baptized, and presented themselves for believers' baptism.

People have come to identify with Baptist principles from many backgrounds; some carry the name *Baptist*, some do not. They have greatly varied ministries. In some areas they have very different perspectives. Baptists still carry the banner of freedom and the Gospel of Christ to a needy world. They have been the most active evangelical group in terms of personal soul-winning for several decades and have led the way in the Christian school movement in recent years. They (along with the Pentecostals and some new-evangelicals) have made fundamentalism a political force in the United States.

At least three Baptists have been elected President of the United States: Harry S. Truman, Jimmy Carter, and Bill Clinton. (Some historical records also list Warren G. Harding as a Baptist.) It is fair to say that none of these would be viewed as a example of a historic, fundamental Baptist. In fact, the policies of President Clinton have been condemned by the resolutions of a number of Baptist groups including the Southern Baptist Convention of which he is a member.

Baptists appear to be at a real crossroads concerning their role in America. Southern Baptists continue to battle over the place of doctrine in their convention. Every year the national media covers the conflicts at the Southern Baptist Convention. Meanwhile, fundamental Baptists have never been more divided. Conflicts over whether the King James Bible is God's perfectly preserved Word, personal and associational separation, and standards of conduct, dress, and music have created many dividing lines among fundamental Baptists. Divisions over personalities of various pastors and evangelists are extremely common. Many Baptist churches are experiencing a decline in attendance as non-denominational "Bible" and "community" churches experience a corresponding growth.

The importance of Baptists politically continues to grow. It is hard to remember that Baptists were once political outcasts. The Democrats count the black Baptist conventions as an important part of their political constituency, and Republicans consider most Fundamentalist Baptists as stalwarts in their camp. Both political parties campaign for influence among Southern Baptists.

Jacob Knapp is remembered as an important influence among Baptist evangelists. Of an Episcopalian background, he became convinced of believers' baptism and presented himself to a Baptist church in Otego, New York. He is remembered as the first full-time independent evangelist (others had worked for Baptist associations). An early campaign (about 1830) was preached in Albany, New York, with 1,500 conversions. He championed a part of the ministry that has proved to be a great benefit to many churches.

In 1886, Dr. Russel Conwell, pastor of Grace Baptist Church in Philadelphia, began a college for those too poor to attend other colleges. This effort resulted in Temple University.

Missionary John Clough went to India in 1864, following several missionaries who had been working among the Telugu people with little success. He contracted with the British government to build a badly needed canal and hired many native Telugu people. Clough organized preachers to minister to the workers on the canal and experienced results far beyond his wildest dreams. On Christmas morning, 1877, more than 2,300 natives presented themselves to his church for baptism. He and six other preachers immersed 2,200 persons in a single day. Within two years they had baptized 8,000 more converts.

In 1884, Baptist missionary Henry Richards began a mission on the Congo River, and within 16 years he had built three churches with a combined membership of over 1,500.

In 1940, a Baptistic preacher, Jack Wyrtzen, founded Word of Life Fellowship and this led to a radio ministry, a camp in upstate New York which serves more than 18,000 campers every year, and missionaries in 27 countries.

Then in Chicago in 1942, a Baptistic preacher named Lance Latham began a camp ministry called Camp AWANA. The AWANA club program grew out of his camp ministry.

In evangelism, education, missions, and youth ministry, Baptists have always been innovators. Their distinctives of the priesthood of all believers and soul liberty have encouraged creativity and independent thinking.

The history of the Baptists proves that the Baptist distinctives work, providing an atmosphere that God can bless and use. The sole authority of Scripture proves an answer for every problem and issue we face.

We Baptists have a heritage of soul-winners like

- John Peck,
- Adoniram Judson,
- Peter of Bruys,
- Henry of Lausanne,
- John Clough,
- William Carey, and
- John R. Rice.

We have a heritage of bold advocates for freedom like

- Arnold of Bresica,
- Isaac Backus,
- Tertullian,
- John Bunyan,
- John Birch, and
- Richard Furman.

We have a great heritage of church-builders like

- Charles Spurgeon,

- George W. Truett,
- Jack Hyles,
- Lee Roberson, and many others.

The Baptist heritage is outstanding! It is a story of faithfulness and evangelism. It is a story of bravery, of sacrifice, and of boldness. It is the story of a "trail of blood."

Our past is glorious. The future has yet to be written.

Young people who are right now getting their training will determine the future.

- They will decide if the future is one of courage or compromise.
- They will decide if the Baptist distinctives will be put into practice or just be given lip service.
- They will decide if the Baptist movement will grow or decline.
- They will decide if the Baptist heritage of freedom is maintained or meekly surrendered.
- They will decide if we have more stories of heroes, of soul winning, of baptisms, of bravery, or if we will surrender the future.

Therefore, it is incumbent upon us to provide them the training they need, properly emphasizing our Baptist heritage, and challenging them to realize that the future of our existence is up to them!

Index

-A-

A History of the Baptists by John
Christian, 168
Abelard, 90
Acts of Pardon, 163
Adeney, 72
adoptionism, 69
Africa, 227
Aidan, 78
Akron Baptist Temple,
Akron, Ohio, 234
Albi, France, 93
Albigenses, 67, 72, 84, 93, 94, 95,
96, 108, 116, 120, 133
alcohol,
see liquor
Alexander VI, Pope, 113
Alexandria, Egypt, 56, 88
Alfred the Great, 79
American Baptist Association,
238, 239
American Baptist Convention,
238
American Baptist Home
Missionary Society,
see Baptist Home Missionary
Society, American
amillennialist, 214
Amish, 161, 170
Amman, Jacob, 161
Anabaptists, 85, 111-117, 130,
131,133, 143-155, 161, 163,
176, 178
Ancient Oriental Baptists, 72
Anglican Church; Anglicanism,
46, 127, 141

Angola, 228
Ankerburg, John, 236
"anti-means" vs. "means"
controversy, 208, 209, 239
Antioch, 88
Apologists, 31
Apostles' Creed, 56
Apostolic Church Fathers, 29-31
apostolic gifts, 30, 32, 45
Appalachian Mountains, 198
Arabs, 71, 227
Ararat, Mount, 70
Argentina, 242
Argentina Baptist Convention,
242
Arius, 56, 57
Arkansas, 199, 238
Arminianism; Arminian doctrine,
45, 175, 179, 188, 240, 241
Arnold of Bresica, 84, 91, 95, 129,
247
Arnoldists, 95, 107, 116, 153
Assemblies of God, 46
Association of Baptists for World
Evangelism, 236
Athanasius, 56, 57
Athenagoras, 31
atonement of Christ (general),
168, 215
atonement, limited, 59
Augustine, Confessions of, 59
Augustine, 58, 59, 77, 82, 83, 126
Aurelius, Emperor Marcus, 50,
125
AWANA, 247

-B-

Backus, Isaac, 187, 193, 195, 247
Bady, John, 101
Bangladesh, 227

Bangley, Thomas, 101
baptism, 16
believers', 114

—249—

-C-

-D-

-E-

-F-

-G-

Galatia, church at, 25
Galerius, 52, 53
Gano, John, 192
Garden Brethren, 150
    see also Anabaptists, German
Gaudentis, 82
Gazari, 72
General Association of Regular
    Baptist Churches (GARBC),
    217-219, 239
general atonement,
    see atonement of Christ
    (general)
General Baptists,
    see Baptists, General
General Missionary Convention
    of Baptists, 206-207, 208
George III, King, 191
Georgia, 207
German Baptists,
    see Baptists, German
German Brethren,
    see Brethren German
Germanic tribes, 72, 75, 77-78, 88
Germany; Germans, 72, 84, 85,
    88, 89, 96, 97, 103, 111, 113,
    114, 115, 116, 119, 121, 136,
    137, 144, 145, 147, 149-155,
    157, 158, 160, 161, 163,

172-173, 174, 186, 224
Gibbon, 72
Gibbs, David, Jr., 235
Glorious Revolution, The, 179
Gnosticism, 32
Gonesius, Peter, 170-171
Gould, Thomas, 185
Grace Baptist Church,
    Philadelphia, Pennsylvania,
    246
Graham, Billy, 220
Graves, James R., 220
Great Revival of 1800,
    see Great Awakening,
    Second
Great Awakening, the, 179, 187,
    188, 241
Great Awakening, Second,
    199
Grebel, Conrad, 143-144
Greene, Oliver B., 236
Gregory the Great, Pope, 78
Gregory VII, Pope, 89
Grevill, Alice, 163
Grosseteste, Robert, 99
Gundulphus, 72
Gunther, Count, 152
Gutenberg, Johann, 122
Gutenberg Bible, 122

-H-

Haiti, 228
Haldeman, I. M., 216
Hamilton, Patrick, 139
Hard-Shell Baptists,
    see Baptists, Hard Shell
Harding, President Warren G.,
    245
Harrison, Thomas, 177
Hart, John, 193
Harvard (University), 185
Hatzer, Ludwig, 149

Helwys, Thomas, 167
Henniger, Dr. Harold, 234
Henricians, 84, 95, 116, 133
Henry IV, King, 102
Henry V, King, 101
Henry VIII, King, 37, 126,
    140-141, 163-164
Henry, Jacob, 168
Henry, Patrick, 132, 188, 193, 194
Henry of Lausanne, 94, 129, 247
Henry of Navarre, 132, 139

Hermas, 29
hermeneutics, 12
Herod, 49
Heroic Age of the Church, 49
Highland Park Baptist Church,
    Chattanooga, Tennessee,
    233-234
Hilarious (converted Lutheran
    pastor), 151
Hindus, Hinduism, 204-205
Hitler, Adolf, 85, 126, 173
Hoffman, Melchoir, 129, 153-154
Holland; Dutch, 67, 86, 101, 116,
    119, 123, 138, 141, 145, 147,
    157-162, 165, 166, 167, 168,
    169, 171, 176, 179, 186
Holmes, Obadiah, 185, 186

Hooper, Bishop, 130, 166
Hosius, Cardinal, 116
Houston, Sam, 200
Hovden, Richard, 101
Howard, John, 210
Howe, Samuel, 176
Hubmaier, Balthasar, 129, 145, 149, 152
Huguenots, 139
humanism, 58, 120
Hungary, 170
Husites, 115
Hus, John, 111-112, 116
Hussein, King (of Jordan), 227
Hut, Hans, 149, 150, 154, 170
Huter, Jacob, 161
Hutson, Dr. Curtis, 232
Hutterrte Brethren, 161
Hyles, Dr. Jack, 233-248
Hyles Anderson College, 233

-I-

Ignatius of Antioch, 29, 30, 50
Illinois, 198
Illinois Friends to Humanity
    Association, 211
illiteracy, 121
immersion,
    see baptism by immersion
independents; independent
    churches; independent

preachers, 53, 55, 65, 66, 75,
    76, 78, 79, 83, 84, 85, 91,
    93-97, 100, 105, 106, 107,
    114, 120, 121, 124, 128, 136,
    138, 144, 165, 168, 171, 176,
    178, 203, 210, 220
independent, autonomous
    churches, 7, 15, 24-25, 42,
    44, 46, 51, 53, 57, 63, 64, 76,
    102, 122, 132, 183

Independent Baptist Fellowship
    International, 241
India, 204-206, 246
Indiana, 198, 211, 214
Indians (North American), 188,
197,
    207
indulgences, 89, 135-136
infant baptism,
    see baptism, infant

Innocent III, Pope, 85, 89, 94, 126
intoxicating beverages,
    see liquor
Iona, 78-79
Irenaeus, 31-32, 50, 129
Islam, 66, 71
Israel, 227
Italy; Italian, 72, 88, 95, 106-107,
113,
    123, 138, 169-170

-J-

-K-

-L-

-M-

-O-

-P-

Peter of Bruys, 91, 94, 129, 247
Petilian, 82
Petrobrusians, 84, 94, 95, 108,
    115, 116, 120, 133
Philadelphia Baptist Association,
187,
    192
Philip, Apostle, 17, 21, 26
Philip the Magnanimous *or* Philip
of
    Hesse, 152
Philip II, King, 159, 164
Philippian jailer, the, 36
Philippines, 227
Picards, 97
Pilgrims, 162, 183-184
Pilgrim Holiness, 45
Pilgrim's Progress, The, 178
plenary inspiration of Scripture, 9
Plymouth Brethren,
    see Brethren, Plymouth

Plymouth Bay Colony, 167
Poland; Polish, 106, 170-171
political unity,
    see unity, political vs.
    doctrinal
Polycarp, 29, 30, 31, 32, 33, 50,
    129
polygamy, 154
Pontifex Maximus, 60
Porter, Ford, 214, 217
post-millennial;

post-millennialist;
    post-millennialism, 177, 214
Potter, Paul and Nancy, 228
pre-millennial; pre-millennialist;
    pre-millennialism, 214, 215
predestination, 44, 59, 131, 138,
167, 203, 208
    see also Calvinism
Presbyterianism; Presbyterians;
    Prebysterian Churches, 11,
    43-44, 194, 209, 210, 245
priesthood of all believers, 7, 9,
    18, 26-27, 30, 44, 46, 47, 57,
    60, 93, 100, 102, 103, 113,
    123, 132, 138, 183, 247
Primitive Baptists,
    see Baptists, Primitive
printing press, 122
private property, ownership of,
    146
Progressive National Baptist
    Convention, 239
Protestant Reformation, The,
    see Reformation, The
    Protestant
Protestant Groups, Traditionalist,
    46
Protestants, 59, 64, 123, 126, 128,
    131, 138, 139, 140, 141, 145,
    146, 159, 164, 165, 166
Pseudo-Christian cults,
    see Cults
purgatory, 89, 136
Puritans, 126, 166, 167, 176, 177,
    184, 185
Pyt, Henry, 171-172

-Q-

Quakers, 141, 166, 176, 185, 195

Quaker Baptists, 186

-R-

Raikes, Robert, 212
Randall, Benjamin, 198, 240
Rauschenbush, Walter, 213

Rawlings, Dr. John, 234
re-baptism,
    see baptism, re-baptism

-S-

of
soul liberty, 7, 9, 18, 26, 43, 44,
45, 93, 100, 108, 123, 132,
183, 191, 213, 223, 247
soulwinning, 232, 233, 241, 245,
248
South Africa, 228, 242
South America, 127, 229
South Carolina, 186, 192, 200,
201, 207
South Korea, 227
Southern Baptist Theological
Seminary, 201
Southern Baptist Convention;
Southern Baptists, 200, 201,
208, 212, 213, 216, 217, 218,
221, 225, 231, 232, 233, 236,
237, 238, 242, 244, 245
Southwide Baptist Fellowship,
241
Spain; Spanish, 123, 138, 159,
164
Spanish Armada, 159
Spillsbury, John, 168, 175
Spurgeon, Charles Haddon, 180,
231, 247
Spurgeon, James, 180

Squire Boone Caverns, 188
St. Bartholomew's Day
Massacre, 139
Stalin, Joseph, 126
Stanley, Charles, 236
Stearns, Samuel, 188
Stennett, Edward, 179
Stennett, Joseph, 179
Stennett, Samuel, 179
Stephanas, 36
Stephen, 27, 49, 129
Stone, Barton W., 210
Straton, John R., 216
Stundists, 170
Succat (Patrick), 76
Sumter, General Thomas, 192
Sunday school, 172, 208, 212,
232, 233
literature, 201
Swabia, 106
Sweden; Swedes; Swedish, 140,
173, 174, 240
Swiss Anabaptists,
see Anabaptists, Swiss
Swiss Brethren,
see Brethren, Swiss
Sword of the Lord, The, 221,
232-233

-T-

Taborites, 112, 113, 116, 170
Tatian, 31
taxation without representation,
191
Taylor, Dan, 180
Taylor, John, 208
Taylor, William, 101
Temple Baptist Church, Detroit,
Michigan, 219, 234
Temple University, 246
Tennessee Temple University,
234
Teprice, state of, 71, 84, 86
Tertullian, 31, 37, 64, 76, 81, 247

Tetzel, Johann, 136
Texas, 200, 238, 241
Textus Receptus, 113
Thailand, 207
The City of God, 59
The Dippers Dipt, 176
The Key of Truth, 70
The Pilgrim's Progress, 178
*The Teaching of the Twelve
Apostles*, 29
Theodora, Empress, 70, 125
Theodosius the Great, Emperor,
54
Theodosius II, Emperor, 83

Theophilus of Antioch, 31
Thomas, John, 204
Thomas Road Baptist Church,
 Lynchburg, Virginia, 234
Tiziano, 169
toleration, religious,
 see religious toleration
Tombalbaye, N'Garta, 227
tongues movement,
 see Pentacostalism
Torrey, R. A., 245

Toy, Crawford, 201
Traditionalist Protestant Groups,
 see Protestant Groups,
 Traditionalist
trail of blood, 132, 133, 248
Trajan, Emperor, 29
Trent, Council of, 116
Truett, George W., 218, 231, 248
Truman, President Harry S., 245
Turming, Richard, 101
Turner, Nat, 223-224
Turner's Revolt, 223-224
Tyndale, William, 102-103, 114,
 140-141
Tzimisces, Emperor John, 72

-U-

Ultraquists, 112
Underground Railroad, 211, 224
Unification, 46
union of church and state, 38, 44,
46, 59, 60, 83
 see also separation of church
 and state
Unitarianism, 199
Unitas Fratum, 112
United States; American, 13, 43,
 44, 46, 54, 80, 84, 86, 87,

103,
 127, 130, 133, 140, 147, 153,
 161, 166, 170, 171, 173, 176,
 183, 189, 191-196, 197-202,
 206-207, 208, 209, 210, 212,
 219, 220, 221, 223-229,
 231-236, 237-242, 243-248
United States Constitution,
 see Constitution, United
 States
Unity (movement), 46
Universalism, 180

-V-

Van der Hayden, J., 160
Van der Sach, Franciscus, 169
Van Impe, Jack, 236
Venner, Thomas, 177
verbal inspiration of Scripture, 9

Vick, G. Beauchamp, 219, 234
Vins, Georgi, 229
virgin birth of Christ, 8, 215
Virginia, 187, 188, 193-195
von Pallant, Werner, 152
Vulgate, Latin, 100, 121

-W-

Waldenses, 67, 72, 84, 94, 95, 96,
 97, 101, 105-109, 112, 115,
 116, 120, 133, 139, 145, 170
Waldo, Peter, 105-106, 129
Wales; Welsh, 77, 102, 185, 187

Wallace, Bill, 226
War for Independence, American,
 84, 153, 188, 191-193, 197,
 198-199
Ward, William, 204

Warren Association, 187
Washington, George, 153, 167, 193
Wassenburg, 152
Way, The 46
Wealthy Street Baptist Church, Grand Rapids, Michigan, 216
Weidman, Peter, 170
Wesley, John, 44-45, 179
Wesleyans, 45

Wessel, John of
   see John of Wessel
Westrup, John, 228
White, William, 101
Whitefield, George, 179
Williams, Roger, 184-185

William of Orange (William the Silent), 21, 86, 132, 138, 159, 179
William III of Orange, King, 86, 132, 159, 179
Wishart, George, 139
witchcraft trials, 96, 186
Word of Life Fellowship, 247
World Baptist Fellowship (WBF), 218, 219, 236, 238, 241
World War II, 173, 229, 244
Wrightman, Edward, 7
Wyche, Richard, 101
Wycliffe, John, 99-101, 111, 141

Wyclifites, 115
Wyrtzen, Jack, 247

-Y-

Yale (University), 185
Yale, David, 185

Yondo, 227
Young, William M., 207

-Z-

Zimbabwe, 228
Zizka, General John, 112
Zoraster, 73
Zwingli, Ulrich, 85, 122, 123,

126, 130, 131, 138, 143, 159

ABOUT THE AUTHOR

 Dr. Phil Stringer is the pastor of the Ravenswood Baptist Church of Chicago. He is a former Bible college president.

He is an active Bible conference speaker having spoken at over 380 churches, camps and schools. He has spoken in 46 states and 13 countries.

He is a visiting professor at Landmark Baptist College (Manila, Philippines), Asia Baptist Bible College, (Manila, Philippines), Dayspring Bible College (Lake Zurich, Illinois), Westwood Baptist School of Missions (Winter Haven, Florida), and the Florida Baptist College (Tampa, Florida). He often teaches as a guest lecturer at other schools. He has taught courses at 16 colleges.

He has written 4 books, 16 booklets, 22 college curriculums, 5 high school curriculums and 1 elementary school curriculum.

He serves on the Board of Directors of Heritage Baptist College, the King James Bible Research Council and the American Association of Bible College Educators. He serves on the Advisory Boards for Bible Nation, First Light Baptist Mission, Shalom Native Mission, The Dean Burgon Society, and the Graceway Bible Society. He is the President of the William Carey Bible Society.

He can be contacted at:

5846 N. Kimball
Chicago, IL 60659
Phone: (773) 478-6083
Email: philstringer@att.net

BOOKS AND DVDS AVAILABLE FROM DR. PHIL STRINGER

$3.00 Books

Majestic Legacy—a look at the 400-year legacy of the King James Bible. The impact of the King James Bible on politics, literature, linguistics, culture and revival.

Biblical English—the distinctive English necessary to convey the original Greek and Hebrew Scriptures into English.

History of the English Bible—the record of the transmission of the Bible into the English language.

In Defense of I John—the most attacked verse in the Bible is I John 5:7. The reasons for including this verse in the text of Scripture are given.

Misidentified Identity—a refutation of the cultic heresies of the Christian Identity movement.

The Real Story of King James—a refutation of the false charges of homosexuality made against King James I.

The Westcott and Hort Only Theory—a refutation of the theory that has challenged the Traditional Text and exerted so much influence on the religious world today.

The Means of Inspiration—a Biblical and historical study proving that the Holy Spirit dictated the words of Scripture.

Many Infallible Proofs—Biblical and historical proof of the existence of Christ and his bodily resurrection.

The Real Story—a look at the missed lessons of history from the Nazis, St. Patrick and others.

Fifty Demonstrations of America's Christian Heritage—fifty proofs of the impact of Biblical Christianity on the development of the culture of the United States.

The Received Text for the Whole World—the importance of having a Received Text based translation for every language of the world.

Ready Answers—an answer to several criticisms of the King James Bible that are advanced by evangelicals and fundamentalists.

The DaVinci Code Controversy—a refutation of the religious and historical themes of the popular books and movies.

$10 DVDs

The History of the English Bible—the history of the Bible from the giving of Scripture to the King James Bible. Originally given at the University of Michigan.

Majestic Legacy—two messages on the 400-year impact of the King James Bible. Originally given at the Immanuel Baptist Church of Coruna, Michigan.

$8.00 Book

The Messianic Claims of Gail Riplinger—a refutation of Gail Riplinger's claims to being a modern-day prophetess.

$12 Books

The Faithful Baptist Witness—a look at the doctrines and history of the historic Baptist movement. A history designed for the average person in the pew.

Gail Riplinger's Occult Connections—a look at the occult teachings of Gail Riplinger's that have infiltrated Baptist churches.

All of these materials may be ordered from:

Dr. Phil Stringer
5846 N. Kimball Ave.
Chicago, IL 60659
philstringer@att.net

All orders above $25.00 are postpaid.

Dr. Stringer is available to speak at conferences on any of the topics covered in his books. Usually this is done on a two-day basis on a Monday and Tuesday. At times, other schedules can be arranged.

CPSIA information can be obtained at www.ICGtesting.com
Printed in the USA
LVOW130858170812

294738LV00001B/44/P

9 780982 223062